In God's Image

Christian Witness to the Need
for Gay/Lesbian Equality
in the Eyes of the Church

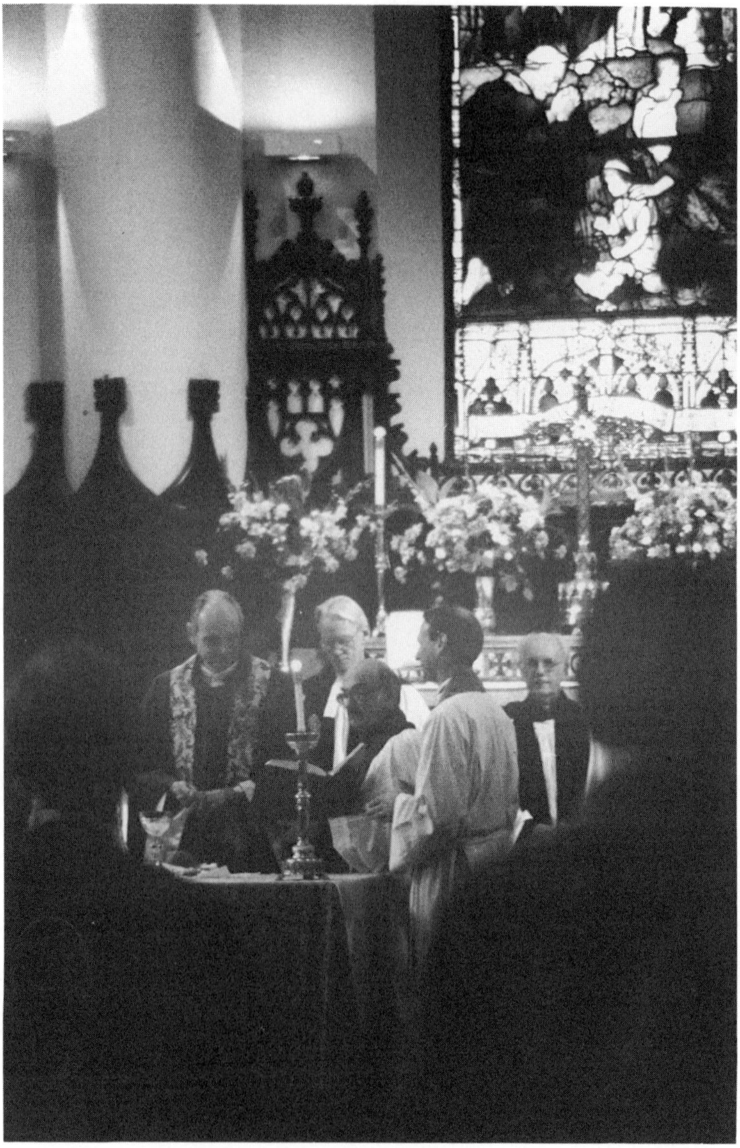

In God's Image

Christian Witness to the Need
for Gay/Lesbian Equality
in the Eyes of the Church

by **Robert Warren Cromey**

Rector, Trinity Episcopal Church

San Francisco

photographs by
Emlyn Wynne

Alamo Square Press
San Francisco

IN GOD'S IMAGE. Copyright © 1991 by Robert Warren Cromey. All rights reserved. Printed in the United States of America. No part of this book may be used or reproduced in any manner whatsoever without permission except in the case of brief quotations embodied in critical articles or reviews. For information, address Alamo Square Press, P.O. Box 14543, San Francisco, CA 94114.

Publisher's Cataloging in Publication Data

Cromey, Robert Warren
    In God's Image: Christian Witness to the Need for
    Gay/Lesbian Equality in the Eyes of the Church;
    Photos by Emlyn Wynne
    Includes index
    1. Homosexuality—Religious Aspects—Christianity.
    2. Gays—Religious Life. I. Title.

BR115   241.66   91-70093
ISBN 0-9624751-2-2

10 9 8 7 6 5 4 3 2 1

To my beloved wife Elizabeth Ann
and my daughters
Leigh, Sarah and Jessica

Almighty God, who created us in your image: Grant us grace fearlessly to contend against evil and to make no peace with oppression, and, that we may reverently use our freedom, help us to employ it in the maintenance of justice in our communities and among the nations, to the glory of your holy name; through Jesus Christ our Lord, who lives and reigns with you and the Holy Spirit, one God, now and forever. Amen

Book of Common Prayer
Page 260

Grant, O God, that your holy and life-giving Spirit may so move every human heart (and especially the hearts of the people of this land), that the barriers which divide us may crumble, suspicions disappear, and hatreds cease; that our divisions being healed, we may live in justice and peace; through Jesus Christ our Lord. Amen.

Book of Common Prayer
Page 823

Table of Contents

Foreword		9
Introduction		13
Chapter 1.	My Life—My Witness	15
Chapter 2.	Meditation	21
Chapter 3.	Attitudes in the Church Today	29
Chapter 4.	Homosexuality—Natural and Normal	33
Chapter 5.	Marriage and Blessings	39
Chapter 6.	Sex In and Out of Marriage	47
Chapter 7.	Forgiveness—We All Need It	53
Chapter 8.	Discrimination	61
Chapter 9.	Unraveling Stereotypes	73
Chapter 10.	Institutional Discrimination	85
Chapter 11.	Homosexuality and Church Unity	93
Chapter 12.	Gay Contributions to the Church	97
Chapter 13.	Ministry to and with Homosexuals	105
Chapter 14.	Effecting Change	113
Index		125

Foreword

This is a powerful, perceptive, compassionate book written by a man truly moved with concern for people, especially those who are victims of injustice and, through our ignorance, relegated to the margins of common life.

Robert Cromey is himself a man willing to change his views when confronted by truth. Thirty-five years ago, while serving as an assistant minister in a church of which I was rector, he came to me for advice. Robert was counseling a homosexual friend, hoping to help him change his way of life. Some years later, Robert told me that he had been shocked at my rather relaxed and permissive attitude toward the situation.

The past three decades have drastically altered common views of homosexuality: from sin, through sickness, to an alternate way of life unchosen by those engaged in it and honorable if practiced in a responsible fashion. Robert Cromey has been a foremost leader in furthering this understanding.

Cromey writes with a prophet's impatience of widespread cruelty and appalling hypocrisy, though sometimes offering little compassion for those who lag behind in the cause, including bishops who must function in a Church still unable to deal constructively with these

In God's Image

issues. This book, based on personal experience with a largely gay and lesbian congregation, will certainly assist readers to face the question with more confidence and less fear.

We see homosexuals as normal human beings living, like the rest of us, according to the nature we have been given: in work and leisure, anxiety and hope, ambition and disappointment, sickness and health, doubt and faith. We discover the unusual strengths such a fringe and outcast group develops to comfort, assist and enjoy one another.

Yet there is no false romanticism in the book, rather a keen understanding of the sin and brokenness in which we all share and the forgiving grace by which we obtain health and salvation—all based on an honest approach to the Bible.

The book underscores the truth that marginalized people rarely achieve justice and redress unless they fight for it themselves and calls on the rest of us to stand with them.

The author and I disagree on certain items: I lay greater stress on underlying Christian oneness and our need for reconciling unity in diversity. I am not comfortable with what sometimes appears as religious consumerism with people selecting churches that meet their own particular needs without awareness of a community of faith. I am particularly uncomfortable with his suggestion that homosexual people exercise financial clout by withholding support to church bodies less than fully committed to their rights.

This is an appropriate time for this book to appear. In an era when populations are increasing beyond the carrying capacity of the environment, why debate over alternate lifestyles? This period of war and massive bloodshed brings to focus a glaring absurdity: how can it be that killing each other in battle or slugging one another to insensibility in a boxing ring is regarded as natural, while to embrace people of the same sex is called perverse?

The Rt. Rev. George West Barrett
Retired Bishop of Rochester, NY

Acknowledgment

The living and the dead have contributed mightily to my life and the ministry out of which comes this book. My parents, the late Rev. Edward Warren and Helen Louise Cromey, gave me my sense of humor and caring for the lives of all people, especially those in need. The late bishops of California, James Albert Pike and C. Kilmer Myers, taught me to use media and social concerns as tools for ministry. Bishop Paul Moore and the Rev. Malcolm Boyd showed me the difference between social action and social service. Bishop George West Barrett gave me the discipline and example to preach the Gospel of Jesus Christ boldly. The Rev. Prof. W. Norman Pittenger taught me to think theologically and ethically, relating Christianity to the world in which we live. The Rev. Harold Lemoine sat me down under a tree when I was a college student and told me he thought I had a calling to the priesthood and that he would pray for me. I thank him too.

Phyllis Lyon and Del Martin, longtime leaders of the lesbian and gay rights movement, witness for me the value of taking a strong public stand and sticking with it until justice begins to seep into the mainstream of American life.

I most joyously acknowledge the members and volunteer clergy of Trinity Church, San Francisco, where I have been rector since November of 1981. They have loved and supported me personally, spiritually and financially these many years. We have fought and bled and died with each other. We have kissed and made up. We are a family. We are broken and healed. We are in the process all the time of learning how to love ourselves, each other and the people of the world.

Finally, I want to thank Bert Herrman, my publisher and editor. First, he took one look at my book and said he wanted to publish it. Second, he took my impassioned ramblings and orchestrated them into a book I am proud to have written. Without Bert, this book would not exist.

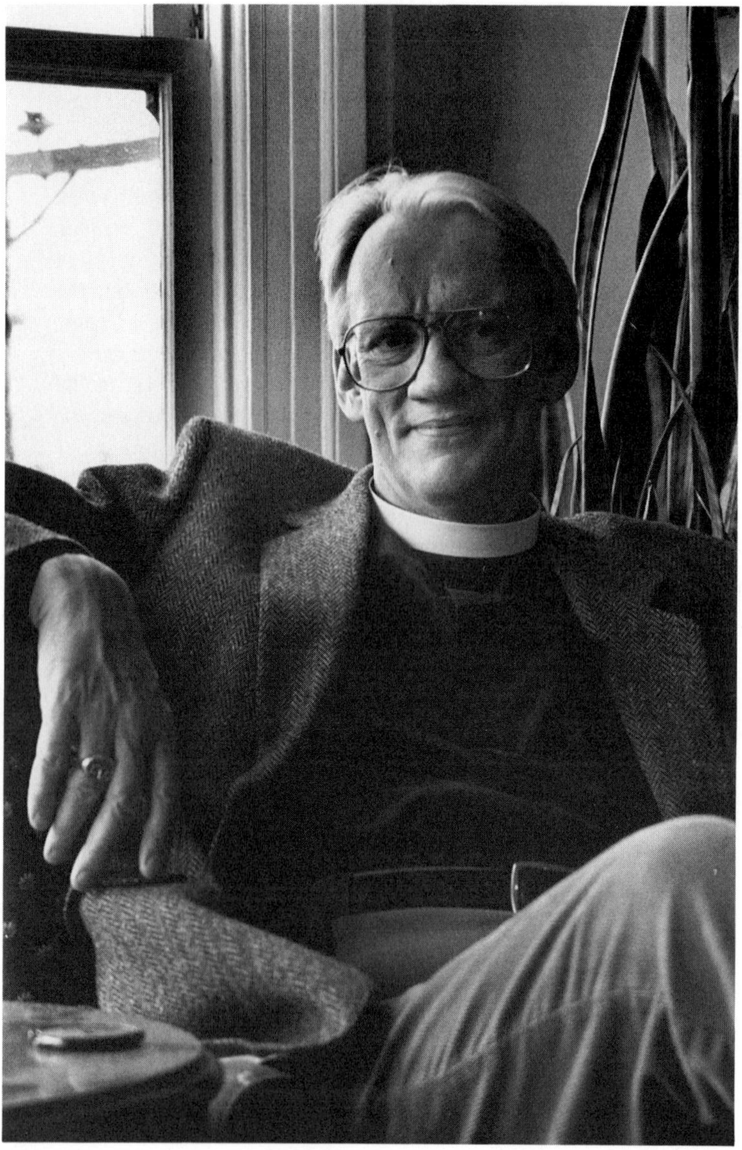

Introduction

The boos cascaded through the Portland (Oregon) Trade Center when I stated that I believe homosexuality is a gift from God to ten percent of the planet's population, that it is a natural, normal part of the lives of millions upon millions of people. This happened during the "Geraldo" television program in May, 1989, on which I appeared as part of a panel of sex-positive clergy. Geraldo and the audience represented conventional morality and they were aghast.

What was I doing there, saying these things?

A priest's job is to speak for the Church. A priest wrestles with the meaning of the Gospel of Jesus Christ to make it clear and relevant to the lives of the people in the parishes and communities of the world today.

At this time, the Church says sexual expression is only for heterosexual people in marriage. I cannot in good conscience speak that word as gospel truth to the Church community or the unchurched population.

The Christian Church stubbornly maintains that all sex outside of marriage is sinful. This outdated view flies in the face of the reality and beauty of human sexuality.

To flatly say that sex between homosexuals, divorced adults, the unmarried elderly, pre-married young adults and for the masturbator is wrong and sinful, is itself wrong and sinful.

Sex between the unmarried can be loving, intimate, caring, sweet, powerful and sanctified. Sex between the married can be careless, hasty, manipulative, cheap and degrading. The position of the Church needs to continue to grow, develop and change so that the full range of human sexuality is seen as a gift from God.

In the 1930s, birth control was disapproved of in the Anglican Church: now it is considered a duty. The Church does come around in time, even in the area of sex.

In this book, I speak not *for* the institutional Church but *to* it. In the 1960s, clergy and lay people spoke to the Church and the country and said that racial prejudice is wrong. Now we must speak and say that prejudice against homosexuals and their sexual practices is wrong. Indeed we must say that prejudice against sex outside of marriage is wrong.

I speak also to homosexual men and women, both in and out of the Church. I affirm their right to express their lives in the way that is natural to them without the need of justifying it to anyone. I speak to the beauty and dignity of their lives and of the sexuality of same-sex lovers. I write against the oppression of homosexuals within the Church and wherever it appears.

Chapter 1. My Life—My Witness

In 1948, Harry Truman defeated Thomas Dewey for president. I was a boarding student at St. Paul's Episcopal School in Garden City, New York. My best friend came tearing into my room and said, "It's terrible, Truman was elected; soon we'll have niggers at St. Paul's."

In 1954, I was a student at the General Theological Seminary in New York City, on the road to priesthood in the Episcopal Church. The U.S. Supreme Court had ruled in *Brown vs. the Board of Education* that separate but equal schools for black people was unconstitutional. I was thrilled, but shocked as many of my fellow (only men in those days) seminarians were outraged, shouting that the decision would ruin the country, the South and the Church, as blacks would be integrated into the larger society.

How could my fellows talk like this? They were Christians; they were studying to be priests of the Church. How could they support oppression in the light of Christ's teachings?

I felt the extent of racial fear and hatred in the liberal North. I had to do something. I became a knee-jerk, bleeding-heart liberal. I took the side of the blacks, arguing for equality and integration.

At seminary, I met the Rev. Trevor Huddleston and heard him

speak of the plight of blacks in South Africa. I read his *Nought for Your Comfort* in 1956, the year I graduated from seminary. In the 1960s I read James Baldwin and the Rev. Dr. Martin Luther King, Jr. Their books shaped my life and my ministry. Each described with passion, pain and hope the oppression of black people in South Africa and the United States.

I remember reading Baldwin's *The Fire Next Time* in my study in San Francisco in the early '60s: I wept at his rage and poetry. I knew then that I wanted to be part of the fight for human freedom and dignity. I knew that as an individual and as a priest I could enfold myself in the cause of justice for black people. It was scary because I had a wife and three young children to support.

In 1964 I went from talking the talk to walking the walk. I was arrested during a sit-in in San Francisco. I remember thinking as I was in the paddy wagon, "Well, there goes my career as a bishop or dean of a cathedral." The protest demanded that automobile dealers in San Francisco hire blacks as salespeople. Four hundred people were arrested, including six clergymen and the movie actor Sterling Hayden.

I was elected to the board of directors of the San Francisco branch of the National Association for the Advancement of Colored People and served for three years. I also went to Selma, Alabama with a couple of thousand other clergy and lay people. Dr. King invited churches and synagogues to join the Southern Christian Leadership Conference in marching from Selma to Montgomery, Alabama to demand voting rights for black people.

As a Christian, I see the gospel of Jesus proclaiming new life and freedom for all people. Resurrection is the symbol of this freedom. Over and over again the Bible calls for justice, yet injustice continues both within the Church founded in Christ's name and in the world at large.

In 1963, I preached a sermon at Grace Cathedral in San Francisco about homosexuals. The Gospel lesson that day spoke of the Christian concern with outcasts. It had somehow occurred to me that homosexuals were not only outcasts, but invisible. I pointed out that they were a silent minority in the Church, ignored except as financial donors. If the sexual orientation or activity of a homosexual priest became public, it was thought necessary to have him removed from his position.

I was interviewed on the radio and in the newspapers and suddenly I was a "queer lover" as well as a "nigger lover." That sermon of mine was patronizing: I suggested that homosexuals needed psychological help, but I did call for love, compassion and forgiveness.

In 1966, I attended a weekend conference of clergy and homosexuals, sponsored by the Glide Foundation of San Francisco. It was a dialogue to discover our mutual humanity. Gay* and lesbian leadership felt the clergy could be valuable allies in the gay rights movement if we got to know each other. We listened to each other's stories, our lives, goals and ambitions.

As I heard of the pain and oppression, as well as the joy and gaiety of homosexuals, I realized that here was another oppressed minority, another group of people deprived of their full humanity "in the land of the free and the home of the brave." It was then I realized that gay rights was a civil rights issue, too.

Together, a group of clergy and gays founded the Council on Religion and the Homosexual. Our purpose was to develop dialogue between straights and gays in the local churches. We felt that if church people could meet openly gay men and women, speak with them, discover their humanity, reconciliation and communication would result.

In 1964, several gay groups sponsored a New Year's Eve costume ball with proceeds to go to the Council. The police were outraged. The vice squad warned us we were being used by the gay community. One asked, "Aren't your wives going to be upset by your hanging around homosexuals?" They even asked us about our

---

* Homosexuals usually find that term too clinical and prefer the expression "gay" or "lesbians and gay men."

theology. They indicated they would make sure that the laws were obeyed at the dance.

When we arrived at the event, police photographers took pictures of all the 500 or so people going into the party. Then the police entered the party looking for law-breakers. Our lawyers tried to block their entrance, saying it was a private party. Two lawyers were arrested for obstructing justice. When the clergy tried to block the police, they just pushed us aside and would not arrest us. Once inside the party, it took the police an hour to finally arrest two party-goers for disorderly conduct.

Now we clergy were outraged. Seven of us called a press conference denouncing the police and their discrimination against gays. They would never invade a debutante ball, an Elk's club costume party; they would never have photographed people entering such events. We witnessed clear anti-gay discrimination and we decried what we had seen.

For the next fifteen years, I remained a staunch advocate of homosexual rights. I took some time off from the active ministry and worked in private practice as a marriage and family therapist until 1981 when I became Rector of Trinity Episcopal Church in San Francisco.

This dying old parish was sorely in need of new life. Here was an opportunity to reach out to singles, gay men, lesbians—the religiously disenfranchised and essentially unchurched. Most churches and synagogues unconsciously focus on families—husband, wife and 2.3 children. My conscious focus was on the unmarried. As a result of my long-standing position and mild notoriety as a gay/lesbian rights activist, many gay men and women came to Trinity. The congregation is now 65 percent gay and lesbian.

My life is full of human beings who love and hate; have good taste and bad; are dull and exciting; conservative, liberal and radical; pretty and plain; black, yellow, tan, red and white—human beings, God's creatures. They make me laugh; they make me cry. I get absolutely furious with some and find myself enamored with others. This is our community.

I am privileged to baptize, present for confirmation and affirmation, bless, counsel, heal, administer Eucharist to and bury many gay men and women. We entertain each other in our homes; we go on hikes, picnics, to the theater, to bars, restaurants and church with each other. We introduce each other to our parents, grandparents, brothers, sisters and children. We weep bitterly over the AIDS-racked bodies of our fellow members and friends. We grieve with the bewildered parents of people with AIDS.

I counsel with people dismissed from the army and navy because they are gay. I talk with veteran soldiers and sailors who have received military honors for heroism, who are gay.

I minister to people who have lost their jobs, their apartments and the bosom of their families because they are homosexual. I know gay men who have been blackmailed because of their sexual orientation. Some have left excellent jobs because they have feared exposure. My parishioners have been beaten, mugged, tossed in jail, harassed and persecuted because they are homosexual.

I have ministered to gays who have beaten people up, forced sex on unwilling partners, been arrested for drunkenness and driving while under the influence of alcohol. They have tossed out lovers who had AIDS. They have chased away lovers who became tiresome and boring.

I am privileged to see homosexual people as real, earthly, sinful human beings. They are not different from my heterosexual friends. They are not "They." They are the crown of creation—human beings—a little lower than the angels. Dust they are; to dust they shall return.

I write this book because I have come to know and love many homosexual people. I have been loved and supported by them as a friend, pastor and activist. The success of the ministry at Trinity is largely due to the time, money and energy of gay men and women.

I am outraged that so many people in our society and Church hate "faggots, queers and dykes." My stomach turns when I hear

In God's Image

Christian people condemn homosexuality as a sin and homosexual people as perverts. I weep when I think of the long road ahead for full freedom. I pray for the souls of my fellow church people who continue to block full freedom for God's children who were given the gift of being drawn in loving and sexual communion with people of the same gender.

Chapter 2. Meditation

Each morning, in my cozy study at home, I open my daily office book. Bound in black leather with gold-edged pages, it fits nicely in the hand. It has traveled with me to England, Ireland and Sweden; to Russia, Uzbekistan and Georgia in the U.S.S.R. as well as around the United States. Each morning, I read the psalms and lessons from the Old and New Testaments. It is a daily discipline of regular readings from the Bible. Over a three-year period I read the bulk of the Bible. Most of the clergy of the Episcopal Church follow some form of this routine.

My mind wanders a lot when I read. My friends, family and parishioners creep into my mind as I pray the psalms and collects. I think of Rodney, a gay man with AIDS. He is terrified of dying. He has hallucinations that someone is trying to get into his small, neat apartment. I pray for him. My mind wanders to people who read the Bible and want to pursue, indict and harm Rodney. He has some right to his paranoia. Self-righteous people are persecuting him. These folks use the Bible as a weapon.

In California in 1987 and 1988, there were ballot measures to

In God's Image

force AIDS testing of homosexuals. These ballot propositions reflect the homophobia* that develops into persecution. The Bible is used to justify such persecution.

There are indeed passages from the Old and New Testaments that appear to condemn homosexuality. Deuteronomy and Romans have such passages. Some scholars say that the passages in Romans refers to pagan male prostitution, not to people living the life of loving homosexuals.**

I am sad so many Christians spend massive amounts of time needlessly judging the behavior of others, often led on by ministers of churches, who muster support by pandering to the bigotry and prejudice of the self-righteous and by using Bible quotes out of context to bash people they hate.

As my mind wanders some more, I think of Pastor Jim, a fundamentalist Presbyterian minister, who came to see me. He wanted to minister to people with AIDS. I asked him if part of his ministry would involve telling people that homosexuality was sinful. Jim said yes, that was his understanding of the Bible's teachings. He said he could love the sinner but condemn the sin. I told him as gently as I could that I would not let him minister to any people with AIDS that I know. I felt bad about turning him down. He wants to minister and help, but he comes from a place of condemnation.

As I try to focus on the Scripture, another image floats into my mind. It is of Pope John Paul II who issued a statement condemning homosexuality and said that people should not be surprised that vio-

---

* Homophobia is a term meaning "fear of homosexuals." Since all hatred and bigotry is based on fear, the term is broadly used for all gay-directed hatred and bigotry.

** For detailed scholarship on passages of the Bible relating to homosexuality, one is well advised to read the definitive work of Yale professor John Boswell:

John Boswell, *Christianity, Social Tolerance and Homosexuality* (Chicago: Univ. of Chicago, 1980).

also:

William Countryman (professor, Church Divinity School of the Pacific), *Dirt, Greed & Sex* (Phila: Fortress Press, 1989).

lence would erupt when people went against traditional thinking about homosexuality. Many of us were outraged that not only did he not condemn violence toward lesbian and gay people, but that he gave an implicit approval to violence. I try not to think hostile thoughts during my meditations. But I confess my failure.

I read my Bible, the same Bible the Pope and the fundamentalists use. I studied Scripture in seminary for three years. I preach using Bible texts. I see a book that tells the story of how God loves his creation, how God loves his people and asks them to obey some basic laws. They disobey; their lives become a wreck; they repent, are forgiven and are promised new life.

The biblical witness shows how we humans fail to love and forgive and so discover pain. The Jesus story says we are loved and cared for by God. That is grace given. We do not even have to earn salvation, health and wholeness. All we need to do is open ourselves to God's love and to serve our neighbors and we are promised wholeness.

As my meditation continues, I recollect how the Bible has been interpreted and reinterpreted thousands of times over the centuries. My credit card swims into my consciousness and I remember that the Bible, if taken literally, clearly condemns usury, the lending of money at interest. I borrow money on the card to buy goods from the store, however, and the credit card company charges interest if I do not pay on time. Our country lends money at interest as a way of helping Third World countries. Our nation would collapse if we took the Bible teaching at face value. Good Christian people have been lending money at interest since the Renaissance.

I yawn, walk around the room and feel the red Indian carpet under my feet. Those carpets are made by people who are paid slave wages. I look at my library and I see the books of Bruce Catton describing the horrendous battles of the U.S. Civil War. Slavery was a major issue in provoking that disruptive massacre. People used the Bible, the Epistle to Philemon and other passages, to justify slavery. Paul tells the slaves to obey their masters. Pro-slavery advocates quoted the Old and New Testaments to justify the economics of buying and selling human beings as slaves in the United States.

Abraham Lincoln's Emancipation Proclamation in 1863 and the 13th Amendment freed the slaves. No one, in or out of the Church, today uses biblical arguments to justify slavery.

I bring my wandering mind and body back to my large maroon leather swivel chair and sit down. On the bookcase is a photograph of my father in a sailor's uniform. It was taken in 1918 while he served in the Navy during World War I. Dad died in 1964. He was a priest of the Church. I grew up as a clergy brat in various rectories in and around New York City.

The only time we ever prayed as a family was grace at dinner. At breakfast and lunch we were on our own. When I was a small boy, Mother or Dad did read us the great Bible stories. When I was confirmed, Dad had my class learn by heart the Apostle's Creed, the Lord's Prayer, the Ten Commandments and the Beatitudes. Never were we hit over the head with the Bible; it was a comfortable part of the stories of our household.

As I thought of Dad, I felt grateful that I was brought up in the liberal, Anglican, Episcopal tradition. I wasn't bugged by fundamentalist rhetoric about the word of God. I wasn't forced to be a creedal or biblical literalist.

I muse about the General Theological Seminary in Manhattan. Its red brick buildings are set on a city block called Chelsea Square. Inside the close, there are large maple and oak trees, green lawns bordered with flowers in spring and summer. Outside, Ninth Avenue roars with trucks, taxis and cars hurtling down the one-way street.

For three years, our class of '56 studied the giants of biblical thought and literary criticism of the Bible. In seminary we discovered the deep religious, spiritual and theological meanings in the ancient stories and myths. We saw the Bible as a library of history, poetry, gospel, letters and prophesy.

Adam and Eve are not historical persons. They are archetypes of all human beings. We, too, lust after the knowledge of good and evil. When we get the answers to our questions, nothing changes. We still have troubles and joys, but we go on lusting for truth. For me to stay hung up on the issue of whether or not Adam and Eve are historical persons robs me of the deeper meaning of the myth.

I love to celebrate and participate in the Holy Eucharist. I love to wear the vestments, my holy clothes, feel the agelessness of the words and action. I love the taste of the bread and wine. I am moved by the solemnity of those who come to the altar to receive the sacrament. I feel rooted in the history of the Church going back in time to beyond time, connected to all the saints, the mystical presence of Christ, back through the mists of mythology—Adam and Eve, Noah and the ark.

In Eucharist, I feel connected to the first fires of the creation of the universe, the planets, the earth and the animal kingdom. I recollect my family and friends—near and far, alive, dead and unborn. It is poetry, mythology, aesthetics, art and religion, all rolled into what we call spirituality.

I cannot rely on reason alone to comprehend these mysteries. I relate to them through my sense of oneness with the universe, my desire to reach beyond myself when I am in need, through my dreams, emotions and intuition. Crass discussions of the literalism of bread and wine becoming body and blood are of little interest to me and my religious life.

Sam is a friend who is a gay atheist. He dismisses God and religion as bogus. When Bill, his lover, was diagnosed with AIDS, Sam cried out, "Oh, please, don't let him die." To whom is he crying? We church folk say God. All we really know for sure is that people cry out beyond themselves when they are in anguish and joy.

I gaze down on my little book so full of the Bible passages assigned for daily reading. I have about ten Bibles around the house and office. Some are old and falling apart. I gave one to my daughter Sarah on her 22nd birthday. It was old and the spine was mended in black plastic tape. At the edges, the red cardboard showed through. It was given to me on my 22nd birthday by my parents. I saw it recently at my daughter's home in Massachusetts.

In God's Image

I have a bright, shiny, all-leather Bible at home, also with gold edges. I keep a bookmark in it. It is a postcard of a bare-breasted, smiling Hawaiian woman offering a fruit basket. I like to shock unwary guests on social occasions.

How often this book tyrannizes people. How often this book about God's love and Jesus' life puts fear and hostility into people's consciousness. The Bible is the central and most important book for understanding Western civilization and the basic human condition.

The Bible is not a rule book, although there are laws in it. When people use it like a rule book they turn it into a club to beat others into submission and obedience. Such people become fanatics, true believers like the rightwing protestant fundamentalist, the authoritarian Roman Catholic, or the Orthodox and Hasidic separatist Jew. Their lives are tyrannized by the book. As a result these groups are also anti-homosexual, against sexual enjoyment and deeply separated from the mainstream of society, hostile to all who differ from them.

Often at Trinity we have Bible study groups. We gather to read the scripture and then reflect on what the passage means to us in our daily lives.

There are people at the groups who have been raised as fundamentalists. They want me, the expert, to give them answers. They want me to give the *right* interpretation. It is hard for them to hear that the interpretation of the Bible changes and varies with new learning and insight.

Many homosexual people cannot understand my statement that the traditional anti-homosexual biblical teaching will change as gay men and women and their allies insist that homosexuals be treated as human beings, as full members of Church and society. They somehow think it does damage to God's word to admit that interpretations of the Bible change over time.

I muse on this book I love. We read it rightly as a book of loving, caring, forgiveness, community—a book proclaiming new life and a new being for all people. Sadly, it remains a mostly unread rule book interpreted by a few fanatics. It is used to exclude and persecute. The Church which I love, whose book is the Bible, continues to be seen as cruel, irrelevant, lacking in passion, pleasure and love.

I get up again, my morning meditation done. I look out the window at the palm tree in the backyard. What a queer-looking tree. It is mentioned in the Bible. In fact, each Palm Sunday at Trinity, we cut some palm branches off that tree to use in the procession. A lot of gay people wave those palm branches. They are good Christians waiting with me for the Church to reawaken to Christ's teaching that all people are welcome in the Body of Christ. No one is excluded.

Chapter 3. Attitudes in the Church Today

In April of 1989, I attended a conference of the Fellows of the College of Preachers in Washington, D.C. Our speaker was the Presiding Bishop of the Episcopal Church, Edmund Browning. He spoke of the missionary thrust of the Episcopal Church. His focus was on the Church overseas, in rural, urban and suburban America, and in the emerging Third World.

I raised the problems of ministry with homosexual people in and out of the Church. I suggested we had a ministry and mission with this ten percent of the population, many of whom are unchurched. He listened attentively. He was thoughtful and sympathetic. A number of the other clergy present commented on this special ministry. In our worship together, people prayed for the success of my ministry with gay and lesbian people at Trinity.

On the last day of the conference, Bishop Browning looked at me for a long moment. He said, frankly, he did not think the problems of homosexuals or their desire to have their relationships blessed was very high on the agenda of the Episcopal Church.

Bishop Browning had delighted and startled many in the Church by saying when he took office, "In our Church there will be no outcasts." But after a number of years touring the Episcopal Church and the Anglican Church, Bishop Browning knows the real position of most Episcopalians towards gays: "It's okay to bury them, but don't ordain them or bless their relationships."

This is also the official position of most of the leadership in the Episcopal Church today. In 1988, the General Convention of the Episcopal Church and the General Conference of the Methodist Church reaffirmed their opposition to the ordination of openly homosexual people in the ministry. Neither dealt with the issue of the blessing or marriage of homosexuals.

The Bishop of California of the Episcopal Church, the Rt. Rev. William E. Swing, has a superb ministry to people with AIDS. He serves on national committees, raises money and is a good pastor to people with AIDS. Yet he does not approve of the blessing of the relationships of homosexuals. He has never stated that he regards homosexual sex as natural or normal. He sticks to the conventional wisdom that all sex outside of marriage is sinful—that all satisfying sexual activity takes place only within the confines of heterosexual marriage.

The convention of the Anglican Diocese of Sydney, Australia, has voted to forbid the baptism of homosexuals, thus denying them all forms of sacramental grace. Gay men and lesbians can't even sing in the choirs.

Some bishops in America, despite the offical ban, will ordain known homosexuals, if they take a vow of chastity. But if the homosexual person is in a lifelong, committed relationship, he or she cannot be ordained because that person is having sex outside of heterosexual marriage. Yet there is no mechanism in the Church for the blessing or marriage of homosexual relationships.

In fairness, I must say there are some bishops who ordain openly homosexual people to the diaconate and priesthood without insisting upon limits on the ordinands' sexual practice. These bishops avoid public recognition of their efforts and do try to bring about change in the conventions of the Episcopal Church.

Conservatively, experts say one-third of the clergy of the Episcopal Church are gay or lesbian. Most are in the closet.* Some vote against the ordination of women as well as openly homosexual people. They fear exposure. They fear advancement will not come if their secret is known. They want bigger and better parishes. They want to become bishops. They go along to get along with the church hierarchy.

By keeping quiet about gay rights issues and avoiding controversy, gay clergy will gain support for their ambitions, but their lives are tied to a very big lie. Like many straight clergy, the closeted gay tells lies in order to get ahead. Hypocrisy in the Church knows no sexual identification.

For the gay parishioner, the situation in the Episcopal Church today appears ambiguous but hopeful. If you are closeted and quiet, you are welcome in the average Episcopal Church, especially in major cities. You can be baptized, confirmed, serve on the vestry, be an usher, sing in the choir, be an acolyte and give money. You could probably even lead a boy or girl scout troop. If you are open about being gay you can do everything but lead the boy or girl scout troop.

In a few parishes your sexuality will be celebrated. You will find classes and seminars dealing with sexuality, relationships, communication skills, crisis, illness and pastoral care. Parish programs will have a focus that includes gay and lesbian concerns.

In most parishes, however, you will seldom hear a sermon, attend a study group or read an article in the newsletter about gay rights. You may be welcome, but you and your concerns will rarely be addressed openly and directly.

If you wish to become a priest or in some way celebrate your relationship, you will meet discomfort or rejection. At best, you will be asked to lie, conceal your sexual orientation and keep the matter of your lover to yourself.

Your homosexuality *is* an issue. Some bishops and commis-

---

* Not publicly admitting their sexual orientation.

In God's Image

sions on ministry (those who help the bishop evaluate potential clergy) will not ask about your sexuality. But they might. Policies about sexual orientation are seldom made public. Some will make inquiry and reject you if you are homosexual.

If, as a typical parishioner, you want to celebrate your relationship with your lover, the bishop may interfere if he hears about it. You may be shunted off to a garden or living room. You can likely get some priest to say some prayers, making you feel like a second-class citizen of the Body of Christ.

Meanwhile, straight people will dress up like toy dolls in fluff and organdy that would make a drag queen blush. They will dress up the church in so many pink flowers and bows it looks like a bottle of Pepto-Bismol. They will swill champagne, gorge themselves with cake and drive off in block-long limos and the bishop smiles, happily preserving the heterosexual sacrament of marriage.

In sum, the Episcopal Church, not unlike most churches, sponsors studies, sets up commissions and issues reports. Yet the Church gives no official support for the vocation of homosexual people to the priesthood. It does not support the blessing of the marital relationships of its gay and lesbian members. On the one hand, it condemns violence toward gays; on the other it makes no significant move to attack the underlying cause of such behavior.

Church leaders will visit you if you are sick with AIDS, bury you if you die of AIDS, but will not allow you to celebrate the monogamous, lifelong commitment you wish to make with your beloved partner. Support for such relationships is an important step toward stopping the spread of AIDS among gay men, but the Episcopal Church is fearful of such a cure.

I received a card[*] the outside cover of which has a benign-looking man peering out warmly, saying "Hi!, I'm a Christian!! Inside the card, the little man becomes an enraged, twisted maniac, screaming, "And I hate gays!! and communists! and unwed mothers! I hate Hindus, vegetarians and anybody who is not a Christian."

---

[*] Produced by Card Shark Productions, Berkeley, CA.

Chapter 4. Homosexuality—Natural and Normal

Tom came over to the flat one evening for a chat. I gave him a Scotch, took one for myself. We sat in the leather easy chairs in the living room. Tom started, "I don't feel queer or perverted. I enjoy using the faggoty games and words but when it comes down to it, I don't feel queer. I bet straight people think of themselves as normal. Well, so do I."

As we talked I realized there were some facts that I believed but hadn't really shared with anyone. Tom and I discussed them at length.

The fundamental fact is that homosexuality is a natural, normal part of creation. A certain portion of the planet's population is homosexual. People are born with the orientation to be erotic and sexually attracted toward people of the same sex as others are attracted to the opposite sex. Homosexuality is not something about which people make a choice. They just *are* that way. Homosexuality thus is not a sin, sickness, perversion or abnormality. It is just the way some people are created.

The psychological world has rethought the matter. The professional associations have taken homosexuality off their list of illnesses. There still are therapists who believe they can change people; the accepted knowledge in the field, however, is that they can only "suppress the behavior of homosexuals, not change their orientation." Suppressed people are time-bombs waiting to destroy themselves and others. Such suppression is a violation of people's humanity, perpetrated by the general society (often aided and assisted by the Church).

Many gay men and women who later in life come to terms with their sexual orientation find themselves forced to leave their spouses and children (and often their churches) to be true to themselves. It will take many years for the churches to take responsibility for the millions of lives they have injured with their self-righteous edicts.

After thirty-two years as a pastor and therapist with thousands of gay parishioners, clients and friends, I am convinced that homosexuality is a good and beautiful part of nature, of God's plan and providence. As good, true, natural, normal persons, lesbians and gay men deserve the full rights, freedoms and privileges that all human beings should enjoy.

What are the grounds for this belief? First, there is an emotional conviction. I have shared immense love, care and affection from gay friends and parishioners over an extended period of time. From this direct knowledge, I derive a conviction and inner certainty. This certainty has become an inescapable commitment.

The first time I ever wrote the words "homosexuality is natural and normal," the words just flowed out of my consciousness onto the paper. It was as if I could not control the writing.

It reminded me of the day when I was seven years old and had been learning to swim. Suddenly, I felt coordinated. My arms pulled in the water. My legs kicked in rhythm and synchronicity with my arms. My head easily turned up for air in a smooth flowing motion. Swimming flowed out of me.

Second, the rational and logical side of myself comes to the fore. There is the argument of sheer numbers. There are 270 million people in the United States. Estimates are that 10 percent of the population is predominantly homosexual.* That is 27 million people. Let's say 10 percent is too high a percentage. Take 5 percent; that's over 13 million who are gay and lesbian. A huge number of people who inhabit our country are being denied full freedom.

The fact that so many of these people live interesting, creative, civilized lives is a telling statement that the abnormality is in the conception of the external community, not in them.

Third, the origins of homosexual feelings lead me to believe in the naturalness of homosexuality. I have asked hundreds of lesbians and gay men when they first knew they were homosexual. Almost all said they knew they were different from a very early age. Some have said as early as four years old. Sexual feelings toward same-sex friends were the earliest felt sexual responses. A few women said they knew they were lesbian after failing to enjoy sex with men and then discovering good sexual feelings with women. Most, however, said they knew when they were very young.

Hearing this over and over again made me realize that no one converted them to homosexuality. It was not anything that someone else did to them. It was a natural, normal part of their life experience. It just happened. It emerged from the way they were created. Their brothers and sisters were heterosexual as were their parents and friends.

Three times when I was a youngster in New York City, I was gently accosted by men. Once in a movie theater, a man put his hand on my leg. I was frightened and left my seat. Another time a male guest in our home crept into my bed. I rolled out of bed onto the floor and he left the room. The third time happened one summer when a man approached me in a restaurant and asked me to have sex with him. I said "No" to these approaches. I had absolutely no sexual excitement in these experiences. I was not converted to homosexuality by these offers. It is clear that I am a cradle heterosexual. I did not choose to be straight. I was born that way. It is the same with gay men and lesbians. They are born that way.

---

* According to many theorists and research of the Institute for the Study of Human Sexuality.

Fourth, diversity in nature points towards homosexuality as natural and normal. Nature is so richly varied. The divisions and subdivisions in animals, vegetables and minerals contain vast combinations of diverse species, colors, densities, flexibilities and sizes. Tints, veins, shapes, liquids, solids, reactions to light and darkness scream the vastness of our universe and spheres of experience.

Those who say that human beings find the perfect expression of sex only in heterosexual marriage fail to notice the beauty and variety of physical and sexual expression in all of nature. Our traditionalists say that men and women can experiment with sex and pleasure only in marriage. Masturbation is taboo. Intercourse before marriage is not allowed. Intercourse after marriage for the widowed or divorced is forbidden. Homosexual sex is sinful. The infinite variety of sexual activity created by nature is turned into a monolithic rigid law of only one right way.

Our sexuality can be expressed in hundreds of different ways, with a wide variety of methods, partners and genders. Variety is not only the spice of life but also the essence of human behavior.

The final argument comes from the Bible and my faith as a Christian. I am not a biblical fundamentalist. I know isolated passages in the Bible condemn homosexuality. I also know of passages that condemn wearing cloth made of fabric from mixed sources, and that command all people who commit adultery be stoned. Most people, even fundamentalists, do not take these passages literally.

The thrust of the Bible is toward loving and obeying God, loving our neighbors, living life abundantly, caring for the poor and the outcast, forgiving each other and working for peace. God created everything and everyone who exists for His purpose. I am not certain what all those purposes are.

When I see the love, caring and forgiveness, joyous living and community among my gay friends and parishioners, I sense the presence of God. When I see the caring and generosity of gay men and lesbians towards those afflicted with AIDS, I see the compassion of Christ. When I see the emergence of gay and lesbian people who claim their dignity, freedom, power and fullness of life, I witness a foretaste of the Kingdom.

Chapter 5. Marriage and Blessings

I was putting some pictures of Uzbekistan, U.S.S.R., in an album after returning from Sabbatical leave. Sitting at the oak dining room table, I glanced out over the blue-tinted city evening. We have a marvelous view of downtown San Francisco.

In the pile of albums, I came across the one holding our wedding pictures. I leafed through it, recalling with warmth and pleasure August 14, 1983, when Ann and I were married. It was the second marriage for both of us. Ann's mother and brothers were there. They flew in from Utah. My daughters had arrived from Boston. The church was packed with friends and parishioners of Trinity. My brother, an Episcopal priest, and his family came from New York. Edwin performed the ceremony and preached at the wedding.

More than half the people at that wedding were gay. They could not easily have the same type of celebration of their relationships. The Church does not allow the marriages of same-sex couples. Bishops forbid the blessing of homosexual relationships. When Ann and I married there was such a groundswell of love, warmth and affection for us; our families and community cheered us as we made vows to each other.

Bishops are odd ducks. They extoll the virtues of marriage, lifelong fidelity and monogamy. They tell us sex outside of marriage is not a good thing. But they're talking about straight people. When they talk about homosexuals they proclaim that gays should be celibate or at least be in committed relationships. In the next breath they say such relationships can't be blessed in the Church. "The Church isn't ready for that yet." "We can't do it in our area." "We must wait for the whole Church to commit to the blessing of homosexual relationships."

Some bishops give secret guidelines for such blessings. Others perform such blessings. Others give tacit approval but don't call them marriages. The less courageous bishops never even face the issues, pretending all homosexuals live in San Francisco.

When I asked one bishop what the difference was between my wedding with Ann and that of a loving homosexual couple, his only reply was that straight people could never accept the word "wedding" used for homosexuals. We'd have to find another word. The "wedding" and "marriage" words are reserved for the straights.

I glanced over my album and there was a picture of Don and Kent holding hands. Kent has already died of AIDS and Don now has the condition. They wanted so much to have a celebration of their relationship in the Church, but they did not want to provoke the bishop, so they backed off. At Kent's funeral, dozens of people spoke of the contribution Kent had made to their lives, both as an artist while he was well, and as a gallant survivor when he was sick. Many spoke to the beauty and inspiration of Don and Kent's relationship and how they had been moved by the couple to enter deeper, long-lasting relationships. We can bury them but we can't marry them!

One of the delights of marriage is the sharing of our love and commitment to our family, friends and community. We want to share our joy. We want the support and undergirding of the Christian Church for our mutual affection. That support empowers us to be together through sickness and in health, in our loving and cherishing.

That support is there if we choose to bring up children. Our gay and lesbian brothers and sisters want that too.

Yes, even children. Many gay people have children by previous marriages. Many are raising their children in single-parent families or in homosexual relationships. Many lesbians and gay men would like to adopt children or have them by artificial insemination. Many such gays would make splendid parents. I have counseled with plenty of rotten parents who are straight.

San Francisco has a municipal court judge who is a lesbian. She and her beloved partner, a respected attorney (and an elected city supervisor), have a baby they are raising. When asked how the child was sired, they smile and say politely, "None of your business." One can tell by the warmth of their personalities and sweetness of disposition that they make splendid female mothers and fathers to that child.

As Ann and I faced each other and recited the words of commitment, we married each other. We were the ministers in the sacrament of holy matrimony. The clergy stand around and say the prayers and sign the papers for the city and county. They celebrate the Eucharist, but the couple does the marrying. Bishops forget that when they forbid the clergy to "marry" homosexual couples. They apparently think the Church does something in the marrying. It is the couple who marry each other.

Harry and James wanted a celebration of their relationship in Trinity Church. James had AIDS. Harry wanted us to bless and celebrate their love before we conducted James's funeral. The service was the Holy Eucharist and exchanging of vows and rings. There was poetry, music, dance and preaching. There were flowers, paper birds, balloons and a splendid party afterward. Everyone was invited to receive the sacrament; most people did. The service went on for quite a while. Harry stopped into my office the next day and admitted it was a bit long. He said, "Well, we wanted to give you a foretaste of eternity."

Like straight weddings, this was a public service. Invitations were sent out. It was announced in the parish bulletin. It was not kept a secret; neither was the story released to the newspapers beforehand.

Several weeks after the ceremony, I talked with Don Lattin, then religious correspondent for the *San Francisco Examiner*. I mentioned I had performed the blessing of a homosexual relationship. He interviewed James and Harry, and a fine story and good picture appeared in the newspaper. The story indicated the blessing had occurred at Trinity and that I was the celebrant.

When the bishop heard about it, his first reaction was that a presentment should be made against me to see if I had violated the canons of the church in such a way that I should be brought to an ecclesiastical trial.

Harry went to see the bishop and got the bishop to agree to drop the presentment plans if I apologized for making the event public and agreed to adhere to the doctrines and discipline of the Episcopal Church. I did so and things calmed down. Under the pressure of the publicity, the threat of trial against me and the unhappy reaction of some relatives, James got very sick and on Palm Sunday, 1988 he died. We had James's funeral at the same altar where his relationship had been blessed.

I am not blaming anyone for his death. James had AIDS, a deadly disease. But the stress and strain around these events certainly helped to hasten his death. This joyous, life-giving, enriching experience of love in Christian community, celebrating a loving relationship, turned into a cause for tension, anxiety and legalistic hassle.

The pictures of joy, laughter and delight in our album are such a contrast to the tension that surrounds the celebration of gay relationships in the Church. I want to weep at the injustice and pain we inflict on gay couples by simple legalisms.

Priests and bishops proudly bless military forces as they go out to kill people. We bless fox hunts, fishing fleets, taxi cabs, debutante balls, pets, missiles and new carwashes. Yet we must not bless people of the same gender who wish to sanctify their relationships

Marriage and Blessings

with the love and support of the Christian community.

Ann and I were each previously married. The laws of the Church used to be that divorced people could not be married again in the Church. This is still the case in the Church of England. In the Roman Catholic Church it is still very difficult to be remarried after divorce. Rules change. What was once impossible in the Episcopal Church is now commonplace. The anti-divorce people still quote the Bible, saying Jesus forbade divorce. The pro-divorce people point out that the Bible is not a rule book; Jesus was not making universal pronouncements on divorce.

The unjust laws of the Church are that same-sex couples cannot marry. Those laws will change over time and, to insure that they do change, we must keep leaning on the Church mothers and fathers who make and change the rules.

When I was divorced in 1969, I was frightened that I would never again get a job as a priest of the Church. At the time, divorce, particularly of a priest, was not considered acceptable.

But people, understanding the evolution of societal conventions, kept pounding at the conventions of the Church to change the rules to keep pace. Many clergy and lay people were getting divorced in the 60s. They were elected to office, to be deputies to conventions. Then the rules began to change.

The situation at hand is no different. The only way the current rules are going to change is for gay people to insist on having their relationships blessed in the churches. When that behavior becomes the norm, then the canons of the Church will change. Lesbian and gay couples must demand to have their relationships blessed. We need priests and bishops who will perform such blessings and marriages. Changes in the law will follow.

Harry and James were married to each other, in every sense the same as Ann and I are married. They shared mutual love. They made vows of fidelity to each other. They agreed to a lifelong union. They promised to be with each other in sickness and health, to love and to cherish, until parted by death. Ann and I do not have a child of our marriage. Harry and James had no children either.

One sunny day shortly before the celebration of their relationship, they came to my office at the church. It is a high-ceilinged room with pointed arched windows and leaded translucent glass. I love pictures and have lots on the walls and on top of the bookshelves. One is a modern icon of Jonathan and David. They are depicted in warriors' garb, but they share a warmth and love for each other. There are lots of reds, browns and yellows in the study.

We discussed some details of the service. Then we shared our experiences of love and relationships. Looking at the marriage service in the Book of Common Prayer, we agreed that it calls for human beings to make a commitment to each other in marriage. It is an act of will to be with each other even when the heat of passion cools to the warmth of love. It takes an act of will to remain with each other when anger erupts and we might feel like walking away. They convinced me they were willing to commit to each other, to keep saying yes to each other, even if they felt like getting out.

Harry knew James had AIDS. Sickness and death was something they had already confronted in their relationship. Because of that, they especially wanted to celebrate their relationship and have the support of their friends, family and community.

I shudder when I think Ann might get killed in an auto, hiking or airplane accident. It is hard for me to entertain the thought of it for more than a few seconds. Yet Harry and James stared death in the face and chose to marry each other anyway.

One Sunday, after there was some criticism in the parish and Diocese, I was in the pink marble pulpit of Trinity. I looked over the congregation of 150 people in a building that seats 750. I thought, we sure have a long way to go to fill up this place. I'd love to see it full of people with a passionate concern for social justice, filled with zeal to assist the world and the Church to become a more fully human place. I spoke, having Harry and James in mind.

I said gay and lesbian people must keep pressing the Church to bless and celebrate their relationships. They must not be afraid of publicity, pressure and stress. Social and religious justice means making sure you can be fully human, fully alive. It is also the way of the Cross. There will be pain in the process.

The Church can only be fully the Church when it is totally inclusive, when it is loving, when it is doing everything possible to include all people into its membership. The Church can only be the Church when it offers all of its members full rights, dignity and opportunities of membership. As long as the Church does selective blessing, selective weddings, it continues to be cruel, picky, narrow, ingrown and ugly.

Simply put, the Church must develop a service for the marriage of same-sex couples. The liturgy must be equal in stature in every way to the celebration of a marriage for straight people presently in the Book of Common Prayer. The Church must encourage lesbian and gay members to enter into holy unions, openly, in public and with the complete love and support of the Christian community.

I began to get hot as I preached on. The Church was deathly silent. The congregation listened carefully. When I stopped, I received a standing ovation. Sermons, even mine, are not normally applauded.

The process of bringing about this necessary change will require risk, education and determination. We will bring justice, love in action, to homosexual people. We risk people leaving the Church. Yes. So be it. We *can* educate people to love gay people. After all, the Church is supposed to be in the love business.

People with AIDS don't have a lot of time to wait for slow legislative processes. We must keep on moving, pressing, striving and forcing change. To say it takes time to make changes plays into the hands of those who fear change, who feel the institution of the Church is more precious than people.

So we will keep leaning on the Church to become itself, the Body of Christ, a community of love, justice and freedom.

Chapter 6. Sex In and Out of Marriage

Jesus said little about sex and nothing about homosexuality. What he did was revolutionize the way human beings were to think about each other. Jesus taught an attitude, a way of being. He illustrated the new approach with parables from the daily life of his times.

Jesus taught that the spirit of our actions is what is important, not a simplistic obedience to a cold law. He taught that the care of people was more important than compliance with codes.

The Judaism of his day was evolving in its understanding of God's law as found in the Old Testament. But the Jews were the people of the law. Much of the personal, trade and agricultural life of the people was regulated by the law. A man was forbidden to have intercourse with his wife when she was menstruating. A man could divorce his wife, but she could not divorce him. Masturbation, the sin of Onan, was forbidden because it was seen as wasting man's seed.

Jesus said he came not to cast out the law but to fulfill it. He proclaimed the inner meaning of the law, not the letter of the law. He healed the sick on the Sabbath day. He urged people to rescue sheep who fell into the ditch on the day of rest. He exalted the hated

Samaritan who showed compassion on the mugged Jew (the Jews regarded the gentile Samaritans as outcasts in Jesus' time). Jesus proclaimed love, compassion, caring and forgiveness as more important than a specific manner of behavior. What is in the heart is what really counts.

Jesus told the woman who had committed adultery to go and sin no more. The sin of adultery is in the betrayal of the relationship, the breaking of the marriage vow and commitment. Sin is not in the sex act itself.

When the Bible was written, the expected lifespan was less than half what it is today. Nobody even dreamed of a world that could be overpopulated. Marriage and children were necessary in order to keep the community going.

Before birth control, sexual expression for a woman meant that she would necessarily have children. Far more than today, it was essential that men be committed to remaining and caring for women and their offspring to assure their survival.

Today, secular law and customs, along with two thousand years of technological advances, have made life considerably different. Women are no longer viewed as the possessions of their husbands. They have a choice whether to work at a trade or stay home, whether or not to bear children. Today, sexuality is no longer allied to the necessity of childbirth, despite the pleas of the Roman Catholic Church that the sole purpose of marital sex is procreation.

Old people and the disabled today discover that they often cannot marry because it would mean losing much of the precious government funding that helps them maintain their existence. Must we label such people's sexual expression as sin and begrudge their relationships our blessings because they cannot afford to marry in the eyes of the law and the Church?

For young people today, life is far more complex than it was two thousand years ago, when it was common to marry not long after puberty. We live in a world where people are expected to have years of training for their chosen profession, years when marriage is often out of the question.

What is more, men and women today are expected to choose their own mates as compared to biblical days when marriages were arranged by the family and a virgin brought a much larger dowry than a girl with experience.

A recent Gallup poll[*] shows that only 33 percent of adults believe that pre-marital sex "is always wrong." Among those who have never married, (to whom this question is most important) that figure drops to 15 percent. But still the Church stands by its ancient doctrine, focusing not on the amount of love and respect in the sexuality, but on the paper that officially sanctifies it.

Today, as in all days, many marriages are more about people "stuck" with each other, than about real love and caring. Impotence, lack of orgasm, brutality, conjugal rape and boredom affect many legally married couples. Church and society pay little attention to these problems. Yet the Church condemns the loving sexuality of unmarried persons. Somehow we have to wake up and realize that the Church is exacting outdated law and falling far short of Jesus' loving teachings.

True, many clergy seldom mention sex or openly disagree with the official teaching of their faith. Few clergy speak much about the specifics of sex in classes or from the pulpit: neither they nor their congregations are comfortable dealing with the subject. It is easier to dismiss sex as something dirty than to take the steps necessary to make it a creative, positive part of peoples' lives.

I have been ordained 35 years and have never taught that sex outside marriage was bad or sinful. In fact, I have encouraged young people to have sex before marriage so they could be sure of compatibility. My encouragement is rarely necessary these days, however, because it is highly unusual to perform a wedding where the couple is not in fact already living together.

In this century, we have learned that men and women, straight

---

[*] George Gallup Jr. and Jim Castelli, *The People's Religion* (NY:Macmillan, 1989).

and gay, have a wide range of sexual and physical needs. Success in a relationship is often dependent on sexual compatibility. To wed without discovering whether you have the ability to satisfy each other sexually is an invitation to a strained and difficult marriage.

For lesbian and gay male Christians, the traditional Church is particularly mean-spirited: not only is their sexual conduct "judged" sinful, but they are not offered the right to have their loving relationships blessed within the Church.

When an unmarried couple has sex, what is in their hearts and spirits when they express their sexuality is what matters. When a person masturbates to relieve physical pressure, or even just for pleasure, it is a fine, God-given gift. I was in my forties before I realized this. Why do we torture youngsters with the notion that masturbation is sinful in itself?

Thoughtful Christians believe that Jesus taught us to go beyond the law to its spirit and inner meaning. We believe we are saved by grace, not obedience to the law. God has already saved us, given us all we need to be whole and healthy. It is not that we do not honor the law. "Stop at the red light," "Do not steal," Do not kill," are good and important laws. The law makes it possible for civilized people to get along together. But personal behavior between consenting adults should not be a matter of the law.

All ethics are thought and rethought as cultures change and develop. Ethics follow behavior. The ethical teachings of religious bodies is slow to change and catch up with the behavior of the people. They will; they always do.

No masturbation; no pre-marital sex; no sex for the divorced, for gay men and lesbians, for widows and widowers; no oral-genital sex; no anal sex. Such are the teachings of most traditional churches, teachings laughed at and ridiculed by most good Christians (at least when the rules apply to themselves or the ones they love).

God created our whole being and saw that it was good. God did not create us, then slap on sinful sex later. We have been bestowed the gift of physical pleasure. Sexual ecstasy can be religious ecstasy, in or outside of marriage. God is in and through our sexuality as God is in and through all of creation. God consecrates and hallows sexuality as it reflects affection, compassion and love, as it celebrates the joy of being alive in God's wonderful creation. So it is, whether we are single or coupled, gay or straight.

Chapter 7. Forgiveness—We All Need It

"Oh, gosh, that door needs a scraping and varnishing. Maybe I'll take it on as a project for myself." The door is large, heavy and has a pointed arch at the top. It has probably hung on the same hinges since the church was built in 1892. I mumble this to myself as I let myself into the hallway leading to my office. I dash up the stairs. Jeff will be arriving in a few minutes. He had called to make an appointment. He said he needed to talk.

On Sunday, I preached that homosexuality is not a disease, perversion or sin. Gays and lesbians are real people, real humans, real persons. They are not freaks. They are human beings with thoughts, feelings, emotions, joys and sorrows. They have religious and spiritual needs, too. They are just like straight people in those areas of life.

Jeff wants to talk about that. He comes into my office. He has on a gray flannel suit, white shirt, rep tie, dark socks and black shoes with side-buckles. He puts his maroon leather briefcase next to the chair beside my desk. I think, "I hope he doesn't forget that when he leaves."

"No matter what you say, Father Cromey, I still feel like a sinner because I am gay. I love sex with my lover. I enjoy caressing his body and making love to him. I love it and then I get a haunting feeling that I am sinning against God. I got that from the church I went to as a teenager."

We talk for a long time. I mostly listen. I assure him that gays are sinners. . . not because of their sexual orientation and practice, but because they are human beings. Christian teaching is clear that we are all sinners; we all miss the mark; we all do things that we ought not do and fail to do things we ought to do.

Jeff would rather have his sin be homosexuality and not worry about the rest of the sins. He doesn't seriously believe that pride and avarice are sins. He doesn't want to hear about the plight of blacks in the U.S. or in South Africa. He doesn't like the notion that he makes decisions as a corporate banker that affect the ozone layer. He'd rather stay lost in the sin of sex. What Jeff needs is a larger vision of what sin is. He gets argumentative and accuses me of getting off the subject.

He's right. I am off his subject. I sense he cannot handle his notion of homosexuality as sinful until he has a broader view of the meaning of sin.

He is shocked when I suggest that the doctrine of sin is a blessed relief. It means we do not have to be perfect, to constantly strive for excellence, hold only the highest standards and never fail. It means we can be exactly who we are. It means we are allowed to make mistakes, have false starts, fall down, be vulnerable and fail.

Jeff says such a notion leads to sloppiness, disorder, chaos and failure. People would never work or attempt to change things.

But by accepting our weakness and failure, I said, we can confess our faults, share them, be forgiven, so we can try again. Then perhaps we can set better goals and move into more realistic paths. It means we can try again and fail again, be forgiven, change again and move forward.

Thomas Edison was not afraid of failure. He tried thousands of combinations of metals while developing the light bulb. He found the one that worked. It carried electricity along the wire and gave off light. Failure and weakness are part of life; they can be used for creativity if acknowledged and used as a springboard into new behavior.

Jeff admitted he demanded perfection of himself. His clothes, his apartment, his lover, his automobile: all had to be perfect. His performance at work strove toward excellence.

He did not live up to his parent's standards of perfection, however. He felt rejected and unworthy and felt they did not approve of the things he did. He went to the wrong college, took the wrong job and hadn't settled down, married and had children.

Of course, he had not told them he was gay. He already knew his parents hated faggots. His father told a story about being to an office party in New York where there were a number of gay men present. He said, "If I had known those people were there, I would have worn my rubber gloves." Jeff was mortified but said nothing.

Jeff felt he had failed his father and mother. "I could never live up to their expectations. I can't forgive myself for failure."

His downcast eyes reflected a man who was missing the mark, who felt unloved and unforgiven.

I suggested I couldn't be of much specific help, but if he hung around the parish, he could talk to others who were working through these same problems. They were learning the blessing, the gift, of accepting themselves as sinners, broken people. By accepting that reality, the limitation of being human, he could learn to feel loved, forgiven and thus begin to reclaim his own being.

I did get on my soapbox again as we talked. I said, "Accepting our sinfulness and our human limitations does not mean you cannot strive for excellence, perfection and high standards. It simply means you can set goals for yourself and choose to act in certain ways. If you fail, you can always start again, make changes and get the job done. But you must be realistic about the possibility of failure and you must be true to yourself."

I pointed out to Jeff that some people choose less than perfection and excellence by the world's standards. Lots of people choose not to accept the standards of parents, school, church, synagogue and society. I have artist friends, small business people and musicians who choose the freedom of working for themselves rather than in the more secure corporate structures.

"Jeff, you believe what the world tells you. You believe that gays are sick, sinful, perverted and abnormal. You buy society's message. You haven't chosen to accept homosexuality as God's gift to you. Just because some folks out there say God hates homosexuality, you certainly don't have to believe it. It is up to you to decide on the value of your own truth."

"Do you really believe that God loves me exactly the way I am?" asked Jeff. "It is hard for me to believe that God could love me when I make love the ways it feels so good to do."

"Yes, Church and society are slowly and agonizingly coming to that conclusion. We, the Church, are getting braver. More people are willing to say clearly that gay people are whole and healthy, sinful people, just like straight people. In fact some of us say God speaks to us through sexual love and love-making. Sexual intimacy is a prayer. It opens us to the creative and emotional drives natural to human beings, that we often repress."

Jeff says, "I guess it will be a while before I can believe that."

"I want to tell you about my friend Tim," I continue. "He is a former Roman Catholic, Jesuit priest. He tells me he feels deeply connected to God and the universe when he is making love with George, his lover. They have been together two years. Both pray and meditate together daily. They attend mass almost daily in a Roman Catholic Church. Their sexual union is a powerful part of their spiritual nourishment.

"One dimension of their religious experience is that feeling of oneness with God, the universe, self and one another. In prayer and meditation, as well as in sex, there is a shift in consciousness to the experience that all is one. Jesus says, 'I and my father are one.' Oneness comes in sex and prayer."

Jeff's eyes widen. He says, "I know that feeling. When I am having sex sometimes, I lose myself and my lover. There is a blending of our bodies, personality and pleasure all into one. I never thought of that as spiritual before."

I get up and stretch. I want a cup of coffee. "Jeff, want a cup of coffee?"

"Yes, I would, please."

"Cream and sugar?"

"Just black, thank you."

"Read this while I get the coffee." I hand Jeff a paragraph I wrote on oneness and sex:

> The sex acts themselves are signs of oneness. My body in your body. Your body in my body. We want to crawl inside the body of our beloved. We desire the body of our lover inside our body. We want the lostness and intensity in the pleasure of orgasm. We want the overall warmth of touch, taste and intertwining. These are outward signs of sex, expressing the inward grace of oneness. Unity with the beloved and God. The Prayer Book has a lovely line about Jesus and us humans. We take the bread and wine at Communion "that He may dwell in us and we in Him."

We drank our coffee in silence.

"I feel horny just reading that. So you really believe I am a sinner, not because I am gay, but because I am a human being and all humans are sinners."

"Yep. Sin has a bad name but it is a good word. I don't plan to ban it from my vocabulary. The human condition is radically imperfect. No one is free from sin. Gay sex is natural and normal and it can be an expression of human love. All sex acts can be used in selfish, destructive ways. But they are not sinful in themselves."

We listen to the traffic go by on Bush Street.

"Jeff, you have to learn to forgive yourself. Sure you've had sex that was promiscuous and hurtful. So have I. So have most people. I have forgiven myself. I feel forgiven by God. You have to forgive yourself, too.

"You have been told all your life that gay is sinful. You have bought that view for yourself. You have been told that the only way you can be forgiven by God and yourself is to confess your sexual practices and give them up forever. Then you can be forgiven. You must become celibate and chaste, before you can forgive yourself. The Pope says that. The fundamentalists say that. The Orthodox and Hasidic Jews say that. The followers of Islam say that. You say that.

"I and others are pressing the Church to get homosexuality off the sin list, just as the psychologists have taken it off the sick list. The only way it will get off the sin list is for gay men and lesbians to stand proud and, along with straight people who have outgrown their prejudice, to keep saying loudly and clearly that homosexual sex is not sinful. We must keep saying it, demonstrating it, insisting on it and pushing the Church hierarchy and councils to open all the doors of the Church and society for human and religious rights for all of God's children."

Jeff squirms uncomfortably, "But I'm not even convinced my gayness is natural. Some part of me sees it as sinful and unforgiveable. How can I forgive myself? How can I work for full freedom for gays, in that case?"

Now, I squirm uncomfortably. What do I say? How do I convince this man to love and forgive himself? I wonder what payoff he gets by hating his sexuality? I decide to use a delicate, sensitive and gentle technique that works with smart people. It is called "stop it."

"Jeff." I assert firmly. "Stop it! Get off it. Right now! Stop thinking that gay sex is bad, wrong and sinful. Stop indulging yourself in self-hatred, pity and loathing. You are a smart guy. Try some new thinking. Say to yourself, 'My homosexuality is a gift to me from God. It is a good and beautiful part of my life.' Say it a hundred times a day until you convince yourself. Sound tacky, corny, too much like positive thinking? You're right. That is exactly what it is. That stuff works for some people who are healthy to begin with. I sense you are a healthy guy, enjoying the pain of your own internalized homophobia."

I shock myself when I talk like this. I'm not so sure it works, but I do think it is worth a try. I think of myself as the pastoral counselor type. I usually listen carefully and assist people to make their own decisions about how they will act and think. I am that way a good deal of the time. But all self-indulgent homophobia does not come from deep-seated emotional problems. Sometimes it comes just from bad habits.

Jeff says, "Well, that sounds good but I don't think I can go that fast. I need to talk to a therapist or spiritual director. I see I need to forgive myself for a lot of things. I need to forgive myself for hating myself, my sexual orientation and certainly some of the abusive ways I have had sex. And my greed level is pretty high. I give little of my money away to help people. I have a nasty tongue sometimes."

He looked like he might cry. "I desperately need to forgive my father and mother, a bunch of former lovers, my employer."

I added gently, "You can also forgive those who oppress you, who dehumanize you and those who try to make you feel guilty."

"I have such trouble forgiving my father; he would come home drunk and beat my mother. I'd try to protect her and he'd whack me," Jeff added.

"Forgiveness can't be perfect either." I said. "Perhaps the best you can do is keep forgiving your father. Maybe if you do it often enough, perhaps his heart will turn and become forgivable. Our job is to keep forgiving. His job is to change and become more human.

"By the way, don't be afraid to forgive God. We all feel oppressed by the mysteries of creation sometimes. It is hard for me to forgive God for allowing the Holocaust, where along with Jews, thousands of homosexuals were killed, too.

"I hate it when my prayers are not answered my way. The God I believe in gives humankind the freedom to torture, wage war and bring suffering to the innocent. I resent a God who creates babies born blind, unwanted, crippled and deformed. But I allow myself to live

In God's Image

with awesome mysteries that confound my comprehension. Sometimes we must allow ourselves to forgive God also."

Jeff says he has to go. I suggest we talk more about these things at another time. We shake hands, then I pull him to my body in a warm hug. He puts his arms around me and sighs deeply. He says, "Thank you, Robert." He picks up his briefcase and leaves.

Chapter 8. Discrimination

The cavernous Gresham Hall, meeting room of Grace Cathedral in San Francisco, has a maroon curtain at one end, blue walls and an unlikely basketball net on one side. This multipurpose room held two hundred people huddled in small groups, eating brownbag lunches. I had just given a speech decrying the failure of the Church to teach about sexuality on the parish level. I had suggested that Church teaching about sex never gave masturbation, homosexuality or sex outside of marriage as an option for Christian behavior.

I was sitting with a married couple, two male priests and a lesbian. The married couple and one priest were charismatic and conservative. The other three were liberal on sexual issues. Kate, the married woman, was tense and fearful as she said homosexuality was against God's word as found in the Bible. Her husband was menacing. He hated the very thought of gay and lesbian life. He mostly glowered and said we had to have standards. The conservative priest asserted that the married state was natural and, therefore, the only right place to express one's sexuality.

I had heard the arguments a thousand times before. I presented my views carefully and in a kindly manner. I could see there was no shaking the firmness of their beliefs. I had hoped Sue would talk about her life as a lesbian, a Christian, a human being. She did not feel comfortable doing that and didn't.

Any hope of people treating each other as human beings will come only as people share the real truth about themselves. In that discussion session, we needed to have a dialogue about who we were as persons. We got nowhere discussing who was right and who was wrong. We got stuck talking about ideas and issues. We never discovered each other as human beings.

Discrimination against homosexual people takes a terrible toll. Kate and George are tight, frightened and use their religion to separate themselves from the world of gay people. Sue walks the tightrope of being in the closet sometimes and out others. She cannot be her real self when she feels compelled to hide her sexual nature.

Discrimination hurts everyone. We hurt ourselves and our neighbors. It is the cause of the spread of AIDS. It took four years to get federal funding for AIDS research because AIDS was regarded as a gay disease. Had it been a disease that affected only aging, male, movie actors, President Reagan would have acted much sooner and with more compassion to provide federal funds for AIDS research and health care. It wasn't until President Reagan discovered that movie star Rock Hudson had died of AIDS that he began to approve of federal action in this crisis, four years after the AIDS epidemic had begun to rage.

In San Francisco, my wife and I live right across the street from Dolores Park. It is two square blocks of open, green space. It rises from 18th Street to 20th Street, where there is a splendid, urban view of downtown San Francisco. There is a playground, always full of children; black, South American, Asian and white. On the terraced slopes, there are often hundreds of sunbathers. It is fondly known as Dolores Beach. Gay men, lesbians and straights bask in the warm sun and cool breezes.

I saw a black teenage boy recently walking out of the park. I was washing my car. As he walked by with his friends, I heard him say, "I'm not coming here anymore, it's full of faggots." He and his girlfriend got into the back seat of a convertible and he put his arm around her. It was an endearing and gentle touch.

I wondered if his teenage juices made him confused. Was his sexuality, so newly blossomed, making him nervous and insecure? Or was he just a bigot? He lashed out at the gay men. Was it compensation for his own vulnerability? Perhaps he had some doubts and fears about his feeling for men. Had he forgotten, or never known, the brutal discrimination suffered by black people?

Instead of dealing with the fear and bewilderment in ourselves, we lash out at others so we can feel strong in ourselves. Some people feel stronger if they have someone to put down and hate. Those who hate Jews, blacks and Arabs are trying to feel strong by debasing others. (The Romans did the same thing to the early Christians.)

We brutalize ourselves when we fail to handle our own hates and fears. We feel better, at least for a few minutes, when we have someone to hate—someone else to blame for the imperfections of the world. But, by definition, people who are full of hate are hateful people.

An acquaintance of mine is the quintessential yuppie—a recent college graduate and fraternity man. He has an excellent job in a brokerage firm. He is charming, handsome and amusing. He tells funny stories putting down women, gays, Jews and blacks. I believe he is well-adjusted sexually. When I told him his jokes made me feel uncomfortable, he rather winsomely said, "I don't really hate those folks, but everyone I know talks like that."

Keeping up. Not being out of step. Being one of the boys. Whatever his reasons, he was still being discriminatory and degrading of other human beings. This behavior ultimately hurts and brutalizes the person who discriminates as well as causing pain to the oppressed minority.

AIDS

In 1982, Donald, the parish secretary, and I were sitting in my office talking about AIDS. We were hearing about it a great deal by then. Donald is a handsome gay man who had studied to be a Jesuit priest. He left because he could not take the vow of celibacy. He knew he was gay and wanted to express his sexuality.

Time and *Newsweek* magazines had just run cover stories on AIDS. Donald was worried. This disease could affect him personally, as well as countless numbers of his friends. I have been wrong a lot in my time, but I have never been more wrong:

"Don't worry, Donald. This will blow over. It'll be like genital herpes and other venereal diseases, gonorrhea and syphilis. In two years, we won't even hear of it again." How wrong! Donald has pointed out the grossness of my error all too many times in the years since.

Recently, in the "prayers of the people," in our Sunday liturgy, Donald read the names of the 27 members of Trinity who have died of AIDS. I personally have conducted the funerals of 20 of those members. In addition, I have done dozens more for people from the community of San Francisco who wanted to have a service at Trinity. As he read the names, we all choked at the sheer magnitude of the pain and suffering we have witnessed in these years since the epidemic began.

Homophobia is why this disease is so widespread among gay men. In 1981 there was plenty of evidence that the disease was caused by a virus. But the only noticeable population affected by the virus was the hated, gay community. Needle users had not yet died in sufficient numbers to be noticeable. Few in America cared that millions of straight people in Africa suffered from the disease.

The Moral Majority lead by the Rev. Jerry Falwell, and other fundamentalists using TV, told listeners this disease was God's punishment on homosexuals. God abhors their sinful, sexual practices. He called homosexuals an abomination in God's sight. AIDS is a disease visited upon homosexuals by a righteous God and they deserved all the suffering they got.

Episcopalians in my parish asked if it was indeed possible that this was God's punishment. Brother Rich, a Franciscan novice, serving the parish as part of his training, taught a Bible class in which this issue came up. He pointed out that lesbians are seldom diagnosed with AIDS. They are homosexual. Was God a sexist only visiting his wrath on gay men? Brother Rich died in 1988 of AIDS.

As the evidence mounted that AIDS was a virus and an epidemic of major proportions was upon us, the President of the United States, the Governor of California and the Mayor of New York City did nothing. The medical and statistical evidence was passed to the highest levels of government. The politicians ignored it. It was not until 1985 that federal money became available for AIDS research.

We were luckier in San Francisco. At the risk of being a sexist, I suggest a woman politician had more heart and compassion than men. The Honorable Dianne Feinstein, Mayor of San Francisco, saw early on that men were sick and dying and she acted. The Health Department took immediate steps to find out the facts of the disease. San Francisco General Hospital set up a special ward for AIDS patients. The staff were recruited and given special training to work with a disease that was unknown, unfamiliar and dangerous.

I have visited that ward all too many times in past years. The care and treatment of the patients is wonderful. The staff treats the patients confidently, with humor and compassion. When 5A is full, AIDS patients have to go to other medical wards. The difference is clear. The care is good, but the spirit and understanding is lacking. The staff in the general wards have no special training to deal with the complexity of problems presented by the AIDS patients.

It also became clear that safe sex education was desperately needed to stop life-threatening sexual behavior among gay men. Use of condoms, to stop diseased semen from entering another person's body, had to be emphasized. Gay male couples needed to be encouraged to solidify and maintain long-lasting relationships. Public health officials, private agencies and the gay weekly newspapers cooperated to make this information available and widespread in the gay community.

In 1982, I encouraged gay and lesbian couples to have their relationships blessed in the Church. I believe it is one way for the Church to support gay men and lesbians in solidifying their relationships and gaining the support of the Christian community in their parishes. It is also an important way to slow the spread of AIDS.

In 1988 the Convention of the Diocese of California passed a resolution expressing support for the development of ceremonies for the blessing of gay and lesbian couples. The vote was 189 to 147. In previous years such resolutions had been soundly defeated.

However, in the meantime, the Bishop of California has forbade me or any other priest from performing such blessing or marriages. He said the Episcopal Church was not ready for such actions and the whole Church had to give permission for the clergy to perform such blessings.

Now, at the very time the homosexual community needed the support of the Church to support lasting unions, the Church leaders become legalistic and suggest waiting. Such permission has not been granted by the national Church. A resolution at the 1991 General Convention could make such unions more possible.

In 1988, factions within the Church lined up to defeat a measure that would have supported homosexual couples in keeping their relationships together. It could help make them stable, long-lasting and perhaps permanent.

At the same time, Roman Catholic and fundamentalist church groups fought safe sex teaching. They refused to encourage homosexual men to use condoms because that appeared to encourage sex that was immoral since it was not leading to procreation.

All this as the AIDS virus was spreading and many gay men did not know they were killing each other each time they made love.

In August of 1990, the National Commission on AIDS, set up by President Bush, reported that federal government research efforts, "fall far short of the mark" and that a "shocking number" of medical practitioners refuse to treat people with AIDS. President Bush chose to separate himself from these findings; they did not hold true with his prejudices and those of his supporters.

The anti-gay feelings in the larger society and in the Church helped spread AIDS, kill people and throttle legislation to provide money for research and medical care for people with AIDS. They have killed and continue to kill.

GAY BASHING

I lead a therapy group of gay men. We were sitting around on the floor of my flat talking about our lives. I asked the group to tell a story about something that frightened them. Tony's hand shot up. He is a flamboyant, charming, gay man. He says, "I was walking down Mission Street and five teenagers were walking on the other side of the street. One shouted at me, 'Hey, you faggot, I'm gonna catch you and screw you in the butt.' I turned the corner and ran like hell."

All too often the gay man doesn't get a chance to run.

I am six feet, four inches tall, weigh 210 lbs., have white hair and have a fairly rugged look. I live near Castro Street, a largely gay neighborhood, with lots of stores, bars, restaurants and services patronized by gay men. I often walk down Castro Street to see and be seen. Many times in the last seven years, a car will zoom by and young men will scream out the window at me yelling "faggot," "queer," and then roar off around the corner.

Several buses pass through Castro Street on the way to other neighborhoods. From the safety of the moving bus, kids scream epithets at gay men walking along the sidewalk.

Straight young men, white, black or Hispanic are the most virulent gay bashers. They patrol gay urban neighborhoods, pick on a lone man they assume is gay, jump out of their cars and beat up the poor fellow. Many deaths and maimings have occurred. Homophobia, discrimination against homosexuals, ignorance and prejudice are the causes of such violence.

Bashings are on the increase since the onslaught of the AIDS epidemic. Young men will say they want to eliminate gays because they are carriers of a dread disease. The same mindless cruelty that says AIDS is a gay disease says homosexuals cause AIDS and they should be wiped out.

Recently, in San Francisco, a teenage boy murdered a gay man, a nearby neighbor. The police were accused of negligence in the investigation. It was alleged that the gay man had seduced the teenager. The juvenile judge decried the murdered man's activities with the boy and made excuses for the boy's murderous attack. Who is on trial here? Is murder justified because there may have been sexual molestation?

In 1986, a gay man died after a beating by some suburban youths who came to San Francisco to do some gay bashing. The mother of one of the accused told the newspapers that the boy had been brought up a strict Mormon, had been told homosexuality was an abomination. She said she wasn't surprised that as a result of such teaching her son would beat up a queer.

My wife Ann was born and raised a Salt Lake City Mormon. Though she had left the teachings of the Church a long time ago, she remained an "ethnic" Mormon until something happened that shocked her terribly. In 1986 a gay man went to his Mormon bishop and reported that he had AIDS and was gay. The bishop's response was to excommunicate him. This story made national headlines.

The party line of the Mormon Church is that the person is excommunicated so that people can pray for the sinner and give him a chance to repent. In this case of homosexuality, it was expected that the boy would be excommunicated so he could be saved. The fact is that the person is forbidden to attend Church, participate in activities, is shunned by Church members and denied the sacrament of bread and water. The young man died a few weeks later. It was after that shocking and cruel treatment of this gay Mormon by his bishop that Ann decided to become an Episcopalian.

The homophobia of the Mormons and other fundamentalists is

mean-spirited and cruel; it amounts to spiritual and psychological gay bashing.

Twice, that I know of, while I was a student in the General Theological Seminary in the 1950s, fellow students were expelled. They disappeared with a day's notice and no explanation to the student body. The rumor was that the seminarians had made passes at young boys. The alleged act of homosexual sex with a youngster resulted in immediate dismissal. No trial by their peers, no investigation, just allegations and judgment. Reputations were smeared and vocations aborted by spiritual gay bashing.

If the accused had resisted or brought action against the seminary, he never would have been ordained nor ever be able to work in the Church.

The sickest psychological gay bashing I ever heard about was in my first parish in the Bronx in New York City. The former rector, a handsome, delicate, married man with children had left the parish after ten years. There were hints of scandal but nothing definite. He and his wife divorced afterward. In 1959, this was "just not done" in the Episcopal Church.

After I became rector, the father of the former rector came to me. He told me he was a former F.B.I. man. He believed his son was a homosexual. He investigated and judged the allegations were true. To protect his grandchildren and daughter-in-law, he felt it was his duty to inform the wife and aid in her separation from her homo husband. The father smeared his son's reputation. His son never again worked for the Church and died a few years later, in his early forties.

THE CLOSET

Ed, a college professor at a local college, came to me while I was a full-time therapist in San Francisco, complaining of writer's block. He'd barely managed to finish his dissertation for his doctorate in history. Publish or perish is the byword in his department, but he just couldn't bring himself to the typewriter. He was the most popular teacher on campus and in his department.

We talked for several sessions and it was clear that Ed was hiding his gayness from the faculty, students, family and friends. He was a closeted gay man. He was hiding his homosexuality from the world. He was living a lie, pretending to his mother that he'd be getting married soon. He was afraid to talk about his sex life, sexual feelings and personal relationships with anyone who might be a threat to his financial or professional life. He had a modest sex life in the bars and the baths but it was separated and lonely. No wonder he couldn't write. He spent all his time and energy hiding.

The therapy sessions became times to discuss how to come out of the closet—that was what he really wanted to do. After many sessions, he slowly came out and discovered the joys of being a free man. As part of his newly found freedom he realized he hated to write and did not want to write. He really wanted to be a teacher. He got a job in another college, where there was no pressure to publish. He has had a fifteen-year, marvelous career as a teacher with an open, gay, personal life.

Lying, deception, half-truths, being constantly on guard are the characteristics of life in the closet. Closeted homosexuals live in constant fear of discovery. I know doctors, dentists, professors, teachers, bishops, priests, deacons, nuns, lawyers, engineers, bankers and real estate brokers who live this way. The most financially successful feel most vulnerable and thus are most deeply in the closet.

Life in the closet leaves a person closed, cool, calculating, emotionally dry and not self-revealing. Intimacy demands that people share themselves with others emotionally, personally and intellectually. Intimacy demands people be open and vulnerable. Closeted gay people are constantly on guard even when they don't need to be.

Peter is a banker. He was in the Army and is still in the reserves. He was married for ten years and is now divorced but good friends with his former wife. He has been gay all his life. He is tall, handsome, humorous and fit. He runs, does not drink or smoke, and has casual, safe sex regularly.

He is conservative politically. His gray flannel suits are impeccable. He attends church each week and gives money to church and charities. He has an elegant, large flat. Peter is in control of his life as a closeted gay man.

No one at his office, the reserves or in his church, knows that he is gay. Neither his former wife, nor his parents, know he is gay. He is careful and cautious, reserved and stiff-necked. He has little personal warmth, even toward other gay men. His sex life is mechanical and pleasure-oriented. He has no desire to be in a relationship. He is likable and fun. But this enormous control and rigidity dehumanizes him. He does not seem like a genuine, whole person. Too much is hidden.

Closeted gay/lesbian people often donate money or time to social services. They give to help people with AIDS and cancer, and to the Red Cross, church and safe charities. They are less likely to give money to work for social change. Causes, political action, legislation for gay and lesbian rights get shortchanged by closeted homosexuals. They fear they will be discovered if they get on lists supporting gay rights. By getting identified with gay rights, they might be accused of being homosexual and might lose employment and money.

It is estimated that at least one-third of the clergy of the Episcopal Church are homosexual. Ninety-five percent of them are in the closet. If most Episcopalians only knew how many of their babies have been baptized by faggots, how many of their children prepared for confirmation by queers: if they only knew how many times they have been visited when sick in the hospital or at home by gay men or dykes, how many of their marriages performed by perverts, how many of their dead had been buried by queens, they'd be shocked beyond belief.

The message is "don't talk about it, keep your homosexuality to yourself, and you'll be ok. Keep lying, keep deceiving, keep withholding who you really are, don't tell the truth and they'll keep you around.

"The ax will fall if you bring a boyfriend to a parish picnic.

You're through if you move your lover into the rectory. It's over if it becomes apparent you are having sex—especially with someone of the same sex. Genteel Episcopalians demand deception, appearances and social niceties."

The Gospel proclaims the truth will make you free.

The evils of discrimination against homosexuals are frightful, dehumanizing and ugly. Homophobia keeps gay men and lesbians impersonal. Homophobia allows straight people to avoid the reality of the sexuality that is around them. Openness about sexuality in general, and homosexuality in particular, makes many people uncomfortable. It forces them to face fears and anxieties about their own sexual makeup.

Chapter 9. Unraveling Stereotypes

"I'm not sure I want my son to have a gay man for a Sunday School teacher," a woman friend remarked recently at dinner. She is a thoughtful, liberal and intelligent woman. She went on to say that she knows in her head that the majority of child molesters are straight men but in her heart she feels uneasy.

The party was small and intimate. There didn't seem to be any room to explore this further. I continued dinner and sipped a nice red wine. I mused on the persistence of stereotyping that homosexuals face.

So many people retain the old bugaboos, fears and prejudices about gays as gospel truth. People's heads are crammed full of misinformation, fiction and downright lies about gay people.

Stereotype number one is that all gay men salivate after young boys and want to introduce them to gay sex. The next jump is that gay men are child molesters and are harmful to young boys. Statistics indicate however that most child molesters are straight men. Gay men who are found guilty of child molesting are usually hiding as straight; they may not even admit their preferences to themselves. Often their victims are their own children.

It was recently revealed that the Roman Catholic Church is spending millions of dollars each year to deal with cases of child molestation by their clergy. These men cannot admit their needs to other adults; preying on innocent children allows them to preserve the lie. Is the sin wholly that of the individual? Or is it the sin of the Church forcing people to disown the nature of their own humanity?

The other day, I was at Joel's house on a parish call. We were talking about how he got involved in gay sex. He said when he was a teenager he was sexually hot for men. At 14 he seduced a 16-year-old boy who had never had sex with another person. He laughed as he described his fumbling attempts to mutually masturbate and have oral sex. It was hardly satisfying but he knew what he wanted sexually.

I have counseled with hundreds of gay men and my findings reflect the scientific data. The vast majority of homosexual men have no sexual interest in young boys and are not interested in having sex with them. Like Joel, most gay men had their first sexual experience with other boys around their own age. They sometimes sought out older, more experienced men to whom they were attracted. Several indicated they even hustled older men for sex.

There is a small organization of gay and straight men who want the laws against child molestation rescinded. Their position is that such laws limit the freedom of children to have sex. While there may be some merit to the idea, very few gay men are interested in the group or even support its existence.

Joel and I were having coffee and his roommate Jerry came in. He said he knew of some gay men who were interested in boys. Jerry, a gay man, said he felt those guys had better obey the law about child molestation. Their activities give the gay community a bad name. Most gay men want the laws about child molestation obeyed by both gay and straight men.

Joel, Jerry and I agreed that straight men should be prosecuted with the same zeal and vigor that gay men are when there is an allegation of child molestation. There is not equal protection under the law in such cases. Gay men are far more likely to be prosecuted than straight men.

Joel is small, dark and very intense. Jerry is tall, dark, handsome and rests easy in his frame. They are not lovers. I asked them what they looked for in a relationship. Jerry said he wanted a man who is interesting to talk with and who is also sexy. Joel said he wanted an intimate relationship where there was a lot of personal interaction and talk as well as physical intimacy. Neither indicated (and I asked specifically) any interest in boys. They are interested in adult relationships in the same way that most straight men are interested in sexual relationships with adult women, not girls.

The second stereotype that many conventional people hold is that being homosexual is an act of will and free choice. They think people choose to go against the norm, indulging in gay sex to shock and flaunt society.

The mother of a young lesbian whom I was counseling told me, "Dorothy is just going with a woman to be different. She could change if she really wanted to." The mother's concept did not match my understanding of Dorothy, of Joel and Jerry or any other gay person I have ever known.

Joel works nights as a computer operator. He walks around the city in the daytime, hears kids call him faggot from the bus. He sees anti-gay graffiti painted on walls. He asks, "Why in the world would anyone choose a life of persecution, physical danger, oppression, ridicule, loneliness, isolation and humiliation? Why would anyone choose that way of life?"

Jerry was brought up in a warm, loving, Roman Catholic home in the Midwest. He went to Catholic schools, college and seminary. He knows the anti-homosexual teachings of his Church very well. He says he knew from the time he was five that he was different. His sexual fantasies, as he was growing up, were all about boys and men. When he masturbated, as an early teenager, he visualized being sexual with other boys or movie actors. He laughs and says, "I even tried thinking of girls but nothing happened. Masturbation was bad enough. But to be a faggot too was more than I could bear as a good Catholic youth. I didn't choose to be gay, but I am glad now that I am."

Sexual feelings emerge from our growth and development. We do not choose our sexual orientation. It chooses us. We do not get to vote about being straight or gay, male or female, left-handed or right, blue-eyed, hazel, green or brown. It might all be in the genes. Time and study will tell. But being homosexual is not a matter of choice.

Many homosexual people try going straight. Sandra is a lovely, petite, school teacher. She married a man in spite of strong lesbian feelings. She was afraid of society's displeasure and discrimination against homosexuals. She had two lovely children, a nice husband and a lousy marriage. She was discontent, irritable and demanding. She realized she was not satisfied personally, sexually nor emotionally by her husband. He was a good man but not a woman.

Sandra divorced and is now in a satisfying lesbian relationship. Her children live with her and her lover; their father has adjusted well to the new situation. Not all such stories have such a happy ending. Lesbians are, as often as not, denied custody of their children and even denied visitation privileges.

There are some gay people who stay in marriages, deflect their homosexual feelings and live happy lives. But people are different. When many gay people try to live the straight life, they suppress their homosexual drives. Marriages are broken, children damaged, parents and friends upset. It is very hard to go against one's sexual nature. Lying, deception and sex outside the marriage relationship betray the integrity of the married state. This is the result of the act of will to go straight. It may work for some, but it won't for many.

It is monstrous to put people in a sexual strait jacket. Sexuality has a natural, normal flow that needs responsibility and discipline. It cannot, however, be denied and thwarted successfully for very long.

No, you don't get to vote on your sexual orientation.

The third stereotype is, "I can always tell one." When I gave a lecture at Mansfield College in Oxford, England, in the summer of

1988, a woman from South Carolina came up to me afterward and said, "I can always tell one, even when they're little boys in fourth or fifth grade."

It is commonplace among macho straight men to say, "I can always spot a faggot after I just take one look."

Ironically gays themselves often perpetuate this foolishness with declarations like: "I can always tell one." or, "We have Gay-dar."

A straight woman member of Trinity met openly gay men and lesbians for the first time when she came to the church. She tells rather winsomely that until she came to Trinity, she never thought she'd met a gay man. Now she knows there were indeed homosexual people in her circle, but they were silent. No one dealt openly with the subject except in a derisive way.

The facts are that no one knows for sure if another person is homosexual. Unless a person says that he or she is gay, there is no way to tell. Psychological, medical, chemical tests do not give clear results. Often delicate straight men and strong or masculine straight women are haunted all their lives by busybodies making incorrect assumptions. People may make good guesses, but that is all they are: guesses.

Homosexual people suit their behavior to their life and work. Executives from Chevron and IBM, stockbrokers, insurance and real estate sales people, football players, movie stars, doctors, dentists, clergy, engineers and housewives may be homosexual and no one knows unless they say they are.

Often gay men and lesbians partake in the colorful gay/lesbian subcultures. Oppression has alienated such men and women from the stifling forms of their oppressors. They take refuge in alternative modes that offer a chance to celebrate their difference and live in truth. Gay/lesbians bars, community centers, churches and synagogues offer a diversity of ways to feel at home with kindred spirits. Some gays feel at home in these settings, others do not.

The fourth stereotype is that gays are promiscuous. Some are and some aren't—just like straight people. Keith is an Episcopal priest from the Southwest who came to visit me at the office. He is a tall, ruggedly handsome man who could pose for a Marlboro ad. He came to talk about the fact that he was tired of hiding in the closet, pretending to be straight. He neither enjoyed his conventional marriage nor was he happy fooling around with casual, gay sex. Keith has two sons, one gay and one straight. They do not know their dad is gay. In the course of conversation, Keith has told me that he has had sex with over five thousand men. Sometimes there were ten a day when the bathhouses were open and appeared to be safe. Keith and I both agree that that is promiscuous sex.

As we chatted, we talked of many men who have had similar and numerous sexual contacts. Before AIDS, many were happy to continue living and having sex in that way. Keith is now in a stable relationship with a man a bit older than he is. He wants to divorce his wife and move in with Kenneth. They wish to establish a long-term, monogamous relationship, but Keith is scared that his promiscuous ways will return to ruin this new and exciting relationship.

It turns out that Kenneth is very conservative sexually. He has had sex with only five different men in twenty-five years. Those men were married and only occasionally had sex outside of their married life. Kenneth, also a priest, felt that having sex with married men was safest. They probably were not going to get hooked on him. There also seemed less chance of contracting a disease and less risk of discovery.

I told Keith that I conducted a workshop in human sexuality for a group of monks from an Anglican religious order. As part of the process we talked about our sexual experiences. One monk, Father Francis, said he was a homosexual, but a celibate: he had never had sex with another person or even masturbated. Keith said it was hard for him to think about such sexual deprivation. There are probably few men, straight or gay, who would disagree.

Promiscuity for some gay men is connected with coming out of the closet, the gay rights movement and gay pride. Gary, dying of AIDS, told me he hated dying. But he said, "Every sexual contact was a political statement. I was free, out of the closet. I was and am myself."

Many homosexual men went through this promiscuous stage of sexual activity. When it became clear, however, that AIDS was spread by unsafe sex practices, men quickly modified their sexual behavior. Many men stopped being so promiscuous and began to seek long-term relationships. Most men began using condoms all the time when having sex. The majority of bathhouses have either closed or are strictly monitored.

Gay men are probably as promiscuous as straight men would be if more women would go along with the idea. As we know, in most cases they will not.

Lesbians, like most women, tend to be more conservative in their chosen number of sexual partners. There are certainly a number of lesbians who are or have been promiscuous, but relationship is, in almost every case, the ultimate goal.

One big issue for lesbians in a long-term relationship is the phenomenon known as "dead in bed." The sex seems to diminish or even die out. It is an issue that is being discussed more and more in sex counseling. Many married people claim the same problem with their husbands and wives.

Patterns of sexuality vary as much among straight people as they do among homosexuals. My friend John told me he lost count after having had intercourse with five hundred different women. Lois told me she had intercourse with over seven hundred men. Often straight men are encouraged to sow their wild oats before settling down to marriage. Such behavior among some straight people does not brand all straights as promiscuous.

Sexual patterns vary tremendously among gay people. Some have tried open and free sex and then gave it up for stable long-term relationships. I know of several men who have celebrated the golden anniversary of being together.

Some men have related to a single partner for a long time and never were promiscuous. Others entered stable, long-lasting relationships but agreed they can occasionally play around. I know Christian homosexuals who feel that monogamy is not necessary for homosexuals. They feel it is a product of heterosexual family guidelines. They predict that open relationships are the wave of the future for homosexual human relationships.

The point in all this is that people are different. People have different sexual drives, desires, appetites, needs and wants. Are gay men promiscuous? Some are, some are not, and sometimes an individual's habits change.

People do not have a choice about having sexual feelings. It is part of the human condition—a delicious part, I might add. But human beings do have choices about how often and with whom they express those sexual feelings.

To label all homosexual men as promiscuous is ridiculous.

The fifth stereotype is that gay men and lesbians want to dress, act and behave as members of the other sex. People believe that if homosexuals live together, one plays the husband and one plays the wife. Some homosexuals believe this too (I'll tell the story of Phyllis and Del in a bit). Confusing this issue are the words transvestite, cross-dresser and transsexual.

A transvestite is a person who feels psychologically impelled to wear the clothes of the opposite sex. They have an inner drive they have trouble controlling or do not wish to control. This is a small group compared to the numbers of cross-dressers. Strangely enough, most transvestites consider themselves straight and relate sexually only or principally to members of the opposite sex.

A cross-dresser is a person, gay or straight, who chooses from time to time to dress for fun or profit in the clothes of the opposite sex. This is often the flamboyant faggot who minces, prances. A person like this drives many gays and straight people nuts. Such is often the intention. He or she may wish to tease and express hostility toward straight people's prejudice against homosexuals.

But many times cross-dressing is a statement of freedom, independence and shear outrageousness. Halloween, New Year's Eve and

Mardi Gras are the three high holidays of cross-dressing. There are male drag queens—mostly gay men who enjoy high camp—who enter contests to get elected "Empress" of their respective cities; the "courts" exist both for fun and as a vehicle to raise funds for political and community service organizations. We had Tatiana, a male drag queen, as a member of our choir for a while. He was upset because he lost as Empress of San Francisco and was assigned as Princess of San Mateo.

We had a Mardi Gras party at Trinity when one of the gay clergy came dressed as "church lady," a character on a TV show. He wore a plain dress; a prim, straw, tiny hat; sneakers, and carried a 1928 Book of Common Prayer. Another of the clergy came in a tight black cocktail dress, hat, veil, fox fur and high heels. His wicked smile peeked out from under his full moustache. Another man came dressed Hollywood style—tight, teal blue, mid-calf pants; sweater, fully bumped, laced with cheap pearls; a bouffant blond wig and sunglasses. It was a great costume party; people had fun.

A transsexual is a man who feels he is a woman trapped inside a man's body, or a woman who feels she is a man trapped inside a female body. After long and careful psychological therapy, a very few people have sex change operations. Christine Jorgenson made international headlines when he had surgery to make his genitals into a woman's in the 1950s.

A woman who comes to Trinity from time to time had lived thirty years of her life as a man. He was a coach and athlete, but he felt something wasn't right. He was not happy; he wanted to be a woman. He went through a lot of therapy and decided to have the surgery and now functions as a woman. She is not now nor has she ever been a homosexual. She never had sex with a person of the same sex. When he was a man, he married and had children. Now that she is a woman she wants to be intimate with a man. While this may sound bizarre to conventional people, these are just folks out there who want to be themselves. They want to speak for themselves and choose how to live their own sexual lives.

Many people think homosexuals play husband and wife in their relationships. Most gay people divide up the chores around the house by interest and talent. One chooses to do the cooking, the other the laundry, one the dishes, the other the budget, one the car maintenance, the other the housecleaning. In most cases, it is absurd to believe one is the "butch" and the other the "femme."

Homosexual people even confuse their roles as they get used to living with each other. Del and Phyllis, long-time lesbian rights advocates, tell this story on themselves. When they began their relationship thirty years ago, they believed the stereotype that one was supposed to be the butch or masculine one. The other was the femme. Del assumed the butch role for a while. She wore trousers and focused on the masculine things around the house like fixing things and handling the money. Phyllis did the cooking, sewing and housework in their cheerful home in the San Francisco hills.

Del realized one day that she really wanted to wear a skirt and do some cooking. But she thought it was not politically correct. She gave up the game playing and began to do and wear what she wanted. Phyllis and Del then divided up the chores by talent and interest rather than the male-female stereotyped gender roles. Even homosexuals get caught up in stereotyping themselves.

The fact is that gay men and women vary as individuals in every way as much as heterosexuals. The only thing they share is their attraction for same-sex companionship and their oppression by Church and society.

Gay people are upset that conventional straight people lump all homosexuals together. They resent that straight people do not take time or interest to see that there are many different kinds of people who are homosexual. The vast majority are not recognizable in society. They dress and act just like everybody else at school, the bank, the office, the church and in the military.

The straight world has in it all kinds of people who play diverse roles and dress in a wide variety of ways. There are suave gentlemen, fat slobs, suburban housewives, gum-chewing shop girls, women who wear furs or curlers in public and punks with green or purple hair. There are single, married and divorced people, many of whom have sex in or out of marriage. We make distinctions between them and honor their differences.

Many straight people have trouble making similar distinctions about homosexual people. They are lumped together as faggots, queers, dykes, transvestites and child molesters. We in the Church are called to see people as individuals, as human beings. We need to go beyond simple-minded clichés and stereotypes and see all people as unique children of God.

Chapter 10. Institutional Discrimination

John-Michael is a gay member of Trinity who works for the federal government. He is program chair of FLAG (Federal Lesbians And Gays). The group meets monthly to support and educate gay men and women employed in government. John-Michael is also active in the Gay/Lesbian Historical Society which gathers historical documents, photographs, manuscripts and souvenirs of gay events, and memorabilia that mark the progress and development of the gay rights movement.

He has invited me to speak to both these groups. We have talked over dinner about how important it is to get gay men and women effectively participating in the political process. Both closeted and out-of-the-closet gays and lesbians can vote, but the burden of standing for office as a homosexual is almost overwhelming. The fact that gay men and lesbians have served proudly and with honor in public office does not seem to daunt people who put their bigotry ahead of their good sense.

Harvey Milk, the first openly gay member of the San Francisco Board of Supervisors, was murdered in his office in City Hall. His successor, Harry Britt, now stands on his own merit and wins his seat without hiding his homosexuality. He has served as president of the Board of Supervisors and even came close to winning a seat in Congress. There are also two lesbians serving as city supervisors.

In San Francisco this is possible. In most places in the United States it would be impossible for an openly gay/lesbian candidate to stand for office, much less win.

There are two openly gay men in the United States Congress, both of whom were voted into office before their sexuality was made public. Both have been reelected to office by their constituencies for their fine work despite intense personal scrutiny and, in the case of Congressman Barney Frank, Congressional admonition for the kind of personal blunder that wouldn't have been sneezed at if a same-gender relationship had not been involved.

In the Armed Services, there continue to be constant witchhunts to remove gay and lesbians from serving their country. In 1989, the Pentagon completed an exhaustive report that showed that gays in the military have been doing an exemplary job and which encouraged the military to allow them to continue their work.* President Bush disowned the report because it was contrary to his personal prejudices and those of his supporters. The witchhunts continue, costing the country millions of dollars and depriving the Armed Forces of thousands of dedicated workers.

Each year, at San Francisco's Castro Street Fair, there is a booth where gay and lesbian police and sheriff's officers hand out leaflets providing information about recruitment into law enforcement. The more homosexuals there are in the police department, the better chance gay and lesbian people have of achieving equal protection under the law. Gay men and lesbians have done an outstanding job as law enforcement officers here and the level of senseless harassment of homosexuals has declined. In other cities, known gay men and lesbians are denied this opportunity.

The *San Francisco Chronicle* reported in November of 1988 that

---

* *Gays in Uniform: The Pentagon's Secret Reports* (Boston, Alyson, 1990).

despite gay officers in their ranks, the San Francisco Police Department was still rife with prejudice and discrimination against homosexuals, as well as against women and people of color. If this is true of San Francisco, how much more prejudice must gays face in more conservative cities?

Discrimination against homosexuals starts at an early age. A gay friend of mine, Jim, teaches in high school. He often sees youngsters singling out a child and calling him "faggot." Jim is afraid to counsel with the boy because he is afraid that he will be accused of child molestation if he raises the topic. In most places, the child has no place to turn.

In 1989, a congressional study was completed on teenage suicide. The original text of this study showed that a large percentage of the suicides were by gay youths. Conservative legislators, made privy to the report before it was released, saw to it that this information was expurgated from the final report—the facts were inconsistent with their personal prejudices.

Recently, I was in my office counseling with a lesbian named Tamara. She is a tall, black woman with marvelous brown skin and deep dark eyes. She talked about her childhood, feeling sexual toward the other girls when they wanted to be close to boys. She spoke of the loneliness of a thirteen-year-old who couldn't talk with anyone about her feelings. She thought her mother and father wouldn't approve. She didn't trust her pastor and teachers. She felt trapped and frightened.

High school youngsters don't like talking to adults about anything. They can be encouraged to talk to someone, a counselor, a trusted friend or a family member about sexuality. Homosexuality in particular and sex in general have to be allowable topics of inquiry. It is tragic that youngsters, and adults as well, are too frozen by fear to talk about homosexuality.

Were it not for her own inner strength, Tamara might easily have added to the youth suicide statistics. In its original form, the congressional study could have been used to promote discussion between teens and trusted adults. It could have saved lives.

In their personal lives, gay men and lesbians are deprived of their most basic rights. In a much publicized recent case, a woman, Sharon Kowalski was severely injured in a traffic accident. Her lifemate, Karen Thompson, was forbidden by Sharon's parents to visit Sharon at the hospital, and the parents kept their daughter hidden away without adequate opportunity for rehabilitation. Karen fought in the courts for visiting rights and proper care for her loved one. She is still fighting to become her lover's legal guardian.

I was talking to two of my parishioners, Sandy and Alexandra, in their lovely home in the Avenues of San Francisco. The cat (I hate cats) jumped into my lap. The patterned red oriental carpet made the living room cozy as we drank tea late one afternoon. These women have been together for fourteen years. Sandy is a banker, Alexandra has been a teacher but stays home now to do painting. She is beginning to sell her work profitably.

They own some income property as well as the house in which they live. They are lesbians and can't marry according to the laws of the state of California. They are denied the automatic, joint property agreements afforded heterosexual couples. They have had to hire a lawyer, no inexpensive proposition, to draw up legal papers assuring that they mutually own all their property. They have had to be specific in their wills that their property will go to the survivor after one or the other dies. This is to protect the survivor from losing the property to blood kin who automatically may have claim on it.

They have also drawn up a durable power of attorney so that in the case of terminal illness, the loving partner can make medical choices about the other. Otherwise a parent or sibling would automatically have the right to make those decisions, leaving out the lesbian partner.

Sandy and Alexandra have taken pains and expense to make sure their rights are protected. They have had to make special legal provisions about health plans, retirement schemes and stock options. Straight people, when they marry, have these rights and privileges granted them automatically by the state.

In the AIDS crisis many gay men have died. Parents swoop in, arrange the funeral, take the body back home somewhere. The bereaved lover is denied the privilege of making decisions for his partner's death and burial plans. Sometimes parents do this with malice because of their anger about their son's homosexuality. Often they take over in the event of their son's death simply because they did not know what plans the deceased had made.

David was born Roman Catholic in the Midwest. He came to live in San Francisco in 1975. A tall, handsome man with a moustache and a slender build, he was a CPA and made good money. He contracted AIDS in 1984. He and his lover Jim attended Trinity regularly. As David's health declined, I often brought Communion to them in their beautiful Twin Peaks apartment.

When David died, his parents arrived. They set up funeral services at a local Roman Catholic Church. Trinity wasn't even notified. Poor Jim had to fight for his own possessions co-mingled as they were with David's. If losing his loved one was bad, David's parents made it worse. This is an all too common story.

When I came to Trinity in 1981, Charles worked for the church a few hours a week, keeping watch while the front doors of the church were open for visitors. He was paid a small amount of money so that it would not interfere with his social security. He stood smartly on the sidewalk in his black verger's gown and became well known in the neighborhood.

Charles lived with George for 35 years. They worked together in the antiques business. When George died of cancer there was little or nothing left over in the business and Charles retired at 65 with only his social security to live on. Had he been legally married to George he would have received additional social security survivor's benefits.

If the man in a married couple is employed by the City and County of San Francisco, the wife is entitled to survivor's benefits. If a lesbian, in a twenty-year relationship, is a city employee, the surviving partner is not entitled to survivor's benefits. The lifelong partners of homosexual Episcopal clergy are not entitled to survivor's benefits by the Church Pension Fund.

There is a bias against gays and lesbians in housing, jobs, adoption services and entrance into universities and professional schools, including theological seminaries. They are discriminated against in the laws of the federal government and in state governments. The God-given rights of all people "to life, liberty and the pursuit of happiness" promised by the Declaration of Independence fall short for those suffering officially sanctioned discrimination.

Along with people of color, Jews and women, out-of-the-closet gays and lesbians are often excluded from the private clubs where so many of the major business and governmental decisions of our country are made. This systematically removes minority people from access to power and hence their fair share of the American dream.

The argument that gay men and lesbians are in some way less capable is ridiculous. When given the opportunity, gay men and women distinguish themselves in the same fashion as anyone else.

A friend of mine belongs to the gay Lion's Club in San Francisco. These people do first-rate social service projects and outdo other Lion's Clubs in fundraising, attendance at meetings and enjoying themselves. When they go to conventions with straight, middle-class America, they are not laughed at or stereotyped—at least not to their faces. They are respected for who and what they are.

Gay men and lesbians have honored themselves in every field where they have made their presence known. Americans are much enriched by the music of Tchaikovsky, Benjamin Britton, Leonard Bernstein, Jerry Herman and Stephen Sondheim. We grow up reading the wonderful works of Walt Whitman, Virginia Woolf, Tennesee Williams and Truman Capote. As novelist Fran Leibowitz put it, "If you removed homosexuals and homosexual influence from what is generally regarded as American culture, you would be pretty much left with 'Let's Make A Deal.'" Where is our respect and gratitude?

Little has been done to rid negative stereotyping of homosexuality in parish churches of the Diocese of California or elsewhere. The clergy leading straight parishes sense that such programs will cause hurt and scandal, and people will leave the Church. They are quite right. Those are the risks. In the 1960s parishes lost members in white areas when movies and videos of black history were shown. Education is hard. Helping people discover the humanity of others is difficult.

Education and consciousness-raising are important but they are not enough. Laws must be changed so that the rights of homosexuals are recognized and made binding on the whole population. Most gay men and lesbians don't care what others think about them as long as they have their full rights and protection under the law.

Black people in the 1960s did not solicit warm attitudes from white racists. Blacks demanded, and are slowly getting, equal treatment under the law. The attitudes of racists and homophobes are far less important than having the freedom to be one's self guaranteed by law. Changes in attitudes follow changes in the law.

In 1987, the Episcopal House of Bishops produced a report about homosexuality with some specific suggestions for Episcopalians. The result of their findings was that the most important way to break down barriers between gays and straights was dialogue.

I decided to test that out. I talked with a couple of Trinity members and we decided we'd make up a team of gay men and lesbians and invite ourselves to other parishes of the Diocese. I sent out invitations to the eighty-six Episcopal churches in our Diocese to invite us to an evening of dialogue and discussion. Not one church responded. Not one responded enough to say, "No."

In San Francisco, the Lay Academy sponsors courses to be given in churches in many areas of religious life. Its purpose is to deepen the religious and spiritual needs of lay people. Courses and seminars are taught by clergy and lay people with special expertise in their field.

Prayer, church history, theology, ethics and parish life are some of the areas covered.

The Parsonage is an organization of gay men and lesbians who were called to minister to people of Castro Street, the gay mecca of San Francisco. The Parsons have been active in supporting the bishop's ministry to people with AIDS and in developing his awareness of homosexuality.

These two organizations were commissioned by the Diocesan Convention of 1985 to develop programs teaching about homosexuality. The Lay Academy has worked with a parish or two in that endeavor. The Parsonage has not done any specific program since that convention. They have a video tape about the Parsonage itself which has made the rounds of some parishes.

Classes and seminars, courses and books, radio and TV programs about homosexual life, behavior, sex and humanity must be produced and disseminated. Our diocese has refused to petition the bishop to set up an educational program for the whole diocese. The bishop has refused to push the two groups who were directed to develop such programs. Progress has been sinfully slow in San Francisco, and even slower in dioceses around the country.

Chapter 11. Homosexuality and Church Unity

My good friend George, who was ordained with me in 1956, recently sent me a letter. In it he wrote, "Cromey, if the Church recognizes homosexual sex as valid and good, the Church will become more divided than it already is."

Here we have the myth of Church unity. The Christian Church is divided into many branches. There are Roman Catholics, Greek, Russian and other Orthodox Churches; Presbyterians, Baptists, Methodists, Mormons and Anglicans. These Churches possess a wide variety of beliefs, doctrines, sacraments, views of the Bible, of ministry and of intellectual freedom.

I wrote back to George and told him the only great principle of unity in the Christian Church today was sexual close-mindedness. Virtually every major denomination is unified under the banner "NO SEX OUTSIDE OF MARRIAGE" and "HOMOSEXUALITY IS SINFUL, BAD AND WRONG."

Christians cannot agree on the nature of Christ, the Church and the Bible. They agree only in being sex-negative. But even these church folk might agree that sex negativity is not enough to be a true basis for Christian unity.

Whenever I teach the confirmation class at Trinity on the doctrine of the Church, I always say there never was Church unity, although there have been times when there was more Church unity than at others—perhaps under Constantine and later under Pope Innocent III.

The disciples split, early on, after Jesus' death. Peter and Paul had factions following them. There was the immediate controversy about whether a person had to be circumcised before he could be baptized into the Church. Paul's epistles indicate clearly that the Churches in Rome, Corinth and Galatia were divided over issues of doctrine, worship and behavior.

It is hard for folks in confirmation classes today to realize that, because Christianity spread so far, so fast and into so many different lands, cultures and climes, Church unity never really existed.

George and I argued about whether or not the Church can be unified in any specific way. My contention is that there is such diversity in human nature, consciousness and attitude, as well as in psychological, cultural and sociological make-up, that no one Christian Church could minister effectively to all people.

Some people need high liturgy, some the quiet of a Quaker meeting. Some need the soul and rhythm of black gospel music, some the somber tones of plainchant. Some people want to be told what to believe, others resent any attempt to be indoctrinated. Some Christians want celibacy, some monogamy and some polygamy. Some people need popes and charismatic figure heads, some prefer the tyranny of democratic assemblies. Some people want bread and wine, others bread and water, some want grape juice and others want none of the above.

George says there can be areas of cooperation and mutual support. Methodists do not have to build churches next door to already exiting Baptist Churches—maybe. He yearns for a time when there will be real dialogue. Some of that is going on and will continue no matter what the sex ethics of some denominations turn out to be.

There is cooperation but not unity.

Church unity is a deep yearning in most Christians. We may be able to find some common ground in Jesus, the Bible and the sacraments, but not all people can find such.

The Church will always be divided. It will continue to break and splinter as people's religious needs become more concrete and specific.

People will leave the churches that see homosexuality and sex outside marriage as valid and good. So be it. It is sad but inevitable. But other people who yearn for sexual freedom and a developed spirituality will come to those churches. They will discover that they become free and loving in churches that accept the realities of sex outside of marriage and the goodness of homosexuality.

Chapter 12. Gay Contributions to the Church

Thomas makes me laugh. He and his lover of over twenty years have the same last name. Thomas took Robert's name because he wanted that symbol of bonding with his beloved. He and Robert are active in the church. Claire is an older woman who was confused by their last names.

"Thomas," she said, "now let me get this straight. You and Robert are brothers."

"No Claire, we're sisters."

"Oh my, I think I'm learning more that I want to know." She nervously walked away.

Ted is dying of AIDS. He became demented and threatened to shoot his lover John. John just held him and waited until the episode passed. When Ted could no longer control his bowels, John would change the diapers he wore. John asked me to come over and visit Ted. Ted was quiet and could only answer yes and no and that very slowly. John cried in my arms. "I feel so helpless."

John makes a lot of money as a graphics artist. He completely supports Ted who has no income, pension or insurance. Ted's lucky:

In God's Image

John is willing to care for him. John provides for nursing while he is at work and then often has his night's sleep interrupted as Ted is often sleepless. Ted is 31, John is 29.

Homosexual people contribute mightily to religion and the truth. The humor of the oppressed and compassion for the sick and the dying are some of the monumental contributions homosexual people have made to our church and society.

A straight woman who is a writer said, "It is really sad. I cannot use the word gay anymore. It has been taken out of the vocabulary by homosexuals. If I say it was a gay old party, people will think I mean that it was attended by homosexuals." Well maybe that would add some life to her parties!

The laughter, jokes, puns and put-downs characteristic of gay life are refreshing. Church life and traditional piety need a strong injection of gay humor. There is no need for church life to be so dull, boring and humorless.

I have attended churches in England, Ireland, Scotland, Germany and all around the United States. There is little humor, laughter or even a hint of the absurd, as the clergy and laity prance around, singing, preaching, kneeling, standing up, sitting down, eating bread, drinking wine and coffee. It is all so humorless, serious and boring.

At Trinity, laughter, applause and good humor make our liturgies human, warm and energizing. There is a part of the liturgy where I do some chanting. One time, the organist flashed me a note, but I missed it by a mile. The choir and congregation chuckled at my mistake and the worship of the almighty God went on unabated.

I was giving announcements from the pulpit one Sunday. I said that people who wanted to say good things about the parish and me could talk with me any time. If they had any complaints they could talk to the organist. With that he leaned on an armful of organ keys and made a mighty "fraaamp," displaying his humorous displeasure with my remark.

My wife is famous for her splendid hats. When Ann and I returned from Sabbatical leave in 1988, at a given signal during the announcement period on Sunday, everyone put on a hat as a way of welcoming Ann back to church after three months away. There were men's hats, women's hats, clergy hats, flowered and velvet hats, safari hats, helmets, watch caps and sailor hats. What a treat!

Gay people also teach the Church compassion. The churches preach compassion; the homosexual community, in these times, acts with compassion. Large segments of the gay and lesbian community have responded to the AIDS crisis with loving kindness. AIDS has killed many young men between the ages of 25 and 40. Men are facing early death for themselves and loved ones even before their grandparents are dead. The first dead person they have ever seen is often their lover.

Jimmy was dying of AIDS. He did not have a lover but plenty of straight and gay people loved him. He was a member of a local San Francisco parish. He got so weak he couldn't take care of himself. His friends arranged around-the-clock care for him. They provided food, medical help, nursing, housecleaning, shopping, cooking and money for their friend. Jimmy's family had disowned him because he was gay. When he died, his extended church family provided a glorious requiem mass and a splendid party celebrating Jimmy's life.

In San Francisco, the AIDS Foundation, San Francisco Hospice, Ward 5A at San Francisco General Hospital and the Open Hand food program are just a few of the groups that have sprung up, organized specifically to help people with AIDS. They have emerged spontaneously from the homosexual community and their supporters to minister to people with AIDS.

The gay political clubs have brought pressure on city, state and federal government to provide funds for research and medical care for people with AIDS. The secular homosexual community has taught the church much about ministering to the ill and helpless.

On Easter morning 1988, I was the celebrant at the early Eucharist at Trinity. It was a grey, foggy morning, contrasting with the church's rich white and yellow floral decorations. I was looking forward to the 11:00 A.M. service with full choir, brass, tympani, organ

In God's Image

and song.

The phone rang in my study. It was Ron.

"Earl died at 4:30 A.M."

"Oh Ron. I'm so sorry. I'll be right over."

Ron and Earl lived just three blocks from the church, so I walked up Gough Street to California and went into the apartment. Earl's sister was there. She was up from Los Angeles; Ron's friends Larry and Mike were there, too. They were the last of the all-night vigil with Earl and Ron. We had a cup of coffee and some cake.

"May I see Earl?"

"Of course."

I went into the bedroom and Earl's soft black features were in repose. He was covered up to his neck in a blue flannel blanket. I thought of how often I had seen him in the hospital with tubes coming out of his body, plugged into machines. I felt relieved that he was dead and out of pain. I said a brief prayer with Ron and I left.

A week earlier, I had seen Earl at U.C. Medical Center. He said he knew the end was near and he wanted to go home. He didn't want to die in the hospital. Shortly after he got back to the two-bedroom apartment he slipped into a coma. Ron asked for help from members of the parish. Thomas organized an around-the-clock vigil for the forty-eight hours before Earl died. People came to be there for an hour or two, so Ron and Earl would not be alone. Food, wine, flowers, magazines, video tapes, cake and coffee were brought in. Folks prayed, sang, swapped stories and laughed and cried as the hours wore on. The clergy came in and out to anoint with oil and lay hands on Earl.

People got punchy and silly. Tension was relieved with laughter and tears. At one point Thomas looked around the bedroom at the six people who were there. Mischievously, he turned toward Earl in bed and said,

"O.K. Earl, enough of this, get out of that bed and straighten up so we can all go home."

Shocked, the room burst into laughter. Earl would have loved it.

Later that morning Ron came to church for the 11:00 A.M. Easter celebration. Earl's body had been taken from his home to be cremated. Ron wept through the service. Friends stood with arms around him, as we sang the glorious Easter hymns. Death and the hope of resurrection were born anew in our hearts as we ministered to Earl and Ron and celebrated the resurrection of Christ at Easter, 1988.

At Earl's memorial service a few days later, I sat in my stall in the sanctuary of the Church. I looked out over the dozens of people who took time off from work to be at the requiem. I thought of the bitter hostility of TV evangelist Jerry Falwell who called AIDS "God's punishment on homosexuals." I thought of the mainline denominations trying to take a "correct" public relations approach to homosexual sex. I looked out and saw homosexual men and women crying, loving, supporting, expressing compassion to Ron and Earl's family. I saw these people so hated, so misunderstood, so ill treated by American society, loving one another. The lesbian and gay community minister to the sick and the dying and bereaved in a manner I have never seen before in thirty-five years as a priest.

I never saw straight people rally 'round so personally to help church members when they were dying. I had never been to a vigil over a dying person with other church people before. I have never seen such compassionate ministry to the sick and dying as I have seen homosexual people give to their brothers dying with AIDS.

James also wanted to die at home. On Palm Sunday, the week before Earl died, there was a vigil around his bed. James was dead. His lover, Harry, did not have James's body moved. His body was covered with a yellow cloth. He was wearing an open-necked shirt. A garland of orange and yellow flowers, a lei, was around his neck. It was evening, the darkened room was lit only with candles. People had brought flowers which were all over the bed and on top of James's body.

James was baritone soloist in our choir. He had many friends in the San Francisco musical world. He and Harry were mystics. I teased them both about being "woo woo Episcopalians." They were interested in Christianity, Catholicism, Buddhism, herbalism, meditation, chanting, white light, crystals and musical comedy. They loved it, enjoyed it, laughed at it, took it seriously and debunked it.

I arrived a few hours after James's death. Fifteen people sat on the floor near the bed where his body lay. They were saying the rosary. There were only two active Roman Catholics in the room, but everyone was saying Hail Marys and Our Fathers in a rhythmic chant. It was vintage James and Harry. Jews, Episcopalians, atheists, singers, dancers, healers, therapists, clergy, gays, lesbians, straights, all saying the Hail Mary. People laughed and cried, told stories, recollections and held each other.

Harry wanted everyone to touch James's head. He said streams of warmth and energy were flowing out of his body.

The room smelled of incense, flowers, candles and warm bodies. After the rosary, some of James's favorite music played softly in the background.

The next day I called Harry on the phone. I said his religious practices must be a great comfort to him now that James was dead. Harry said he was tired of that religious stuff, so on this day he was listening to some musical comedy.

A few days later a splendid requiem was celebrated at Trinity. The service began with the Kaddish, the Hebrew prayer for the dead, recited by James's Jewish friends standing around his casket.

I always invite everyone in attendance to partake of the consecrated bread and wine of our Christian Eucharist if they feel so moved. I also tell the congregation that it is okay not to come to the communion rail. All are welcome, no one need feel bad if they choose not to participate.

At communion that day I was deeply moved to see eight Jewish men in yarmulkes receiving communion in order to be in concert with Harry and his lover James, the musician, the Episcopalian, the gay man who had died of AIDS.

As I gave out the bread of Eucharist, the mystical presence of

Christ, I saw the homosexual community being the Church. They minister to the dying and the bereaved. They take the beloved forms of the Church and use them creatively to minister to all human beings. They bring new life and new being to the Church.

Not once in thirty-five years in the ministry have I ever seen the dead body at home with flowers and garlands, incense, candles, music, song, prayer and laughter.

When my mother and father died, we had the body removed from the house, taken down to the funeral parlor, where embalming, cosmetics and the sticky sterility of the funeral home disguise death as sleep. Then we had a nice service at the church, then burial in a cemetery with no headstones: neat, clean, respectable, sanitized and unreal.

The religious needs of the homosexual community must and can be met by the Church. But we, the Church, have much to learn from the action and sensitivity of the homosexual community.

Chapter 13. Ministry to and with Homosexuals

Richard called one day from Santa Cruz, California. He is a priest of the church, but was then in 1980 working in a dog grooming salon. He said he appreciated an article I wrote on gay/lesbian rights for one of the church magazines. He was quite amazed to learn I was not gay. He was cheered that a non-gay person would take a strong public stand on homosexual rights. I told him I felt called to this ministry and added, "I'll be damned if I know why."

When Richard moved to San Francisco, he attended a parish where the rector delegated Richard to the choir in the balcony, refused to allow him to wear his clerical collar to church and suggested he keep in the background for a while. That rector was a gay priest. He treated Richard like a second-class member of the Body of Christ. He was not allowed to celebrate the Eucharist, preach or just hang out in ecclesiastical garb.

I became rector of Trinity in November of 1981. Richard called and asked if we could talk. I invited him to be a volunteer priest at Trinity, to take a turn in celebrating the Eucharist, preaching and helping with the pastoral and teaching load. He agreed and has been

In God's Image

with us ever since.

Since then, I have had 14 volunteer assistants. All but three have been homosexual men, priests of the Episcopal Church and formerly employed by the Church. To a man, they have been discriminated against because they are openly gay. Two have died of AIDS. Two are sick with the disease. At least one is HIV positive.

These gay men joined me in my ministry at Trinity because they respected my general stance about gay and lesbian rights. They are not paid for their ministry as we do not have enough money to hire clergy assistants. (No women priests have come to Trinity during these years, although I would love to include them in our ministry.) These gay men work with me and our members of the congregation to provide a ministry for all our parishioners.

People often ask, "What should the Church be doing about homosexuals?" Put that way, the question reflects the problem. Baptized homosexuals *are* the Church. They are members of the Body of Christ by their baptism. The perception that we have a homosexual problem shows how thinly we view the Church. Homosexuals are not outside the Church; we are all members of the Church together.

Rick has been a priest for 25 years. When he came out as a gay man, he was pressured to leave his parish, get a divorce and move from Denver. He says, "I am relieved that I do not have to hide anymore. I am sad for all the deception and the pain my wife and family went through.

"I really just want to work for the Church. After all I am a born and bred Episcopalian, as were my family before me. I've baptized countless babies, performed dozens of weddings, visited the sick, counseled the bereaved and buried the dead. I taught children and adults about Christianity and preached a million sermons. I helped raise half a million dollars to build a parish hall. I served on the school board of the city. The only thing that seems important in the eyes of my bishop is that I'm gay. It really is frustrating."

Shirley is a deacon of the church and a hospital chaplain. She has an outstanding record as a minister to people with AIDS. A remarkable teacher and storyteller, she is in great demand as a speaker and seminar leader. She is openly gay and lives with her lover.

"When the chaplaincy of the local Episcopal hospital came open, I thought I'd have a shot at it. I applied. It soon became clear they were not going to hire me even though I had been in the neighboring city hospital for eight years. The board chose a straight man from another city to take the job. Sure he's competent and a good fellow.

"I love the Church and the ministry in hospitals, but some day I'd love to work in a parish. I think my chances are pretty slim, but I'll hang in there as the Church lurches toward full freedom of opportunity for all people."

The facts are that some Christians discriminate against other Christians who are lesbian and gay human beings, baptized persons. The facts are that many homosexuals want full equality in the Church. The facts are that lesbian and gay Christians simply do not want to be discriminated against because of their sexual orientation. The facts are that homosexual people demand their right to be treated as individuals, as full and equal members of the Body of Christ, the Church.

The 1978 Lambeth Conference report says, "Today we do not expect everyone to conform to a norm—a sort of average humanness—but rather to rejoice in variety; so the status and rights of homosexuals are being reconsidered...

"Homosexuals ask for recognition of the fact that their homosexual relationships can express mutual love as appropriately for the persons concerned as a heterosexual relationship might for others."[*]

Homosexuals today, like the blacks of the 1960s, demand the Church to be the Church. Blacks and homosexuals, women and all repressed minorities demand the Church be a loving, forgiving, caring, inclusive community.

Those of us who work for social justice have a ministry *with*

---

[*] Report of the Lambeth Conference, 1978 <C 10> p. 64-65, section E. The Lambeth Conference is an international conference of Anglican bishops held every ten years.

homosexuals, not *to* them. We listen carefully to groups of homosexual people within the Church, especially Integrity, a national organization of gay/lesbians Episcopalians. We listen to individuals, groups and all who have an interest in struggling for the freedom of oppressed people. We work in concert; we work alone; we work as we are called to the achievement and maintenance of justice for homosexual people.

In the late 1960s black power advocates pushed white liberals aside and rejected any help from "whitey." Twenty years later black power folks are less vocal. Blacks and some whites still press for economic justice for black people in our society.

What does ministry with homosexuals look like in the Church today? First, in parishes and dioceses there must be a movement of people—gays and straights—with shared goals and objectives. These goals will include the ordination and the hiring of homosexual people without prejudice because of their sexual orientation, and the marriage or blessing of homosexual couples in the Church. There will be other goals.

I recently had breakfast with Thomas and Robert at their home. They are in a twenty-year-plus relationship. As they maneuvered around the kitchen making a hearty breakfast of bacon, eggs, toast, butter, coffee, cream, sugar and preserves, they talked about their plans for the day. I thought how natural, easy, normal, relaxed and conventional their life is. How could people hate them if they saw them making breakfast for their parish priest on a Saturday morning with the smell of bacon and toast and coffee in the air?

My wife Ann and I went sailing with Jane and Sally. Jane is a physician and Sally a high school teacher. They are lesbians and members of Trinity. They sailed the boat in the cool, stiff breezes of San Francisco Bay. We ate egg sandwiches and shared beers and coffee. We chatted about children, church, politics and vacations. Once in a while we even mentioned sex and Jane told one of her raunchy stories—doctors seem to know a lot of them.

Ministry with homosexuals means people being with people.

We assure each other we will work for the full rights of all people, especially homosexuals, in church and society. It means insisting those rights be granted. It means patiently educating, leading along, those people who wish to oppress homosexuals.

This ministry with homosexuals must include ministry to the special needs of gay men and lesbians. They must unlearn some sleazy theology: "God hates homosexuals." "God disapproves of sex." "The Church is an exclusive club rather than an inclusive community." Homosexuals need to learn how to get out of the closet—to be honest with themselves, their neighbors and their God. Many need also to relearn that the Christian Church is a place of love, not betrayal. They need to relearn the sanctity of worship.

All people need to learn more about good love, joyful sex, intimate relationships and positive communication skills. Gays learn from earliest memory that God is against sex pleasure and especially same-gender sex pleasure. God is presented as a gendarme out to nab the sexual activist.

This fundamentalist notion of God must be outgrown. God is love. Wherever there is love there is God. God is present in love, sex and pleasure whether it is a one-night stand, a brief genital encounter or a lifelong committed relationship. God's love is present and smiling on our pleasure, our feeble attempts to be loving and find love. God's love appears as we enter relationships and make commitments.

People are welcome to grovel in their anti-sexual piety, but the love of God is broader, deeper, higher and more powerful than our petulant narrow views of God's providence.

Rethinking their outworn and jaundiced position on homosexuality can give all people an opportunity to look anew at their own sexuality—to reopen themselves to this natural, joyous part of life. At the same time, we can challenge ourselves through feminist and gay/lesbian literature to stretch beyond our limited and constrained thinking about gender. Men can give back to themselves the right to feel, touch and care. Women can open the possibilities of their lives to their loftiest dreams.

In God's Image

Ministry with homosexuals means helping people see the Church as an inclusive community dedicated to following the rabble-rousing rabbi, Jesus. The good news of the gospel is that the Church is for everyone who wishes to go through the initiation rite of baptism to join up.

Ministry includes helping gay and lesbian people to get out of the closet. The more people accept Church and society's demand to be quiet and hide their sexuality, the more people remain stuck, frozen, tense and hiding.

Mary doesn't want her family to know she is a lesbian. She is an engineer and doesn't want the people at the office to know. She is limited in her self-assertion, appears quiet, mousy and lacking in spirit and energy. She hides her sexuality and she ends up concealing her true personality.

Zal was curate in a Southern parish. "I was in charge of the youth group and the music program of the church. I was popular with the kids and parents. The choir worked well together and we made beautiful music. I wrote an article for one of the church magazines and came out in that piece. I was fired from my job, not for incompetence but because of sexual prejudice.

"I expect the Church to be a place that is open to all human beings. I want the church to love us all, no matter what our sexual makeup. I expect the Church to stand up for gay and lesbian people the way it has, at long last, for black people."

Michael was a priest for only ten years. Because he was openly gay he could never gain full-time employment in the Church. He went from diocese to diocese and bishop to bishop looking for any kind of work in the Church. He never was hired.

"Being a priest doesn't mean you have to have a job in the parish," he would often say. "I'm a priest no matter what I work at. I was a bartender and bouncer in gay bars for awhile. I did work as a volunteer chaplain in an AIDS ward. I was among the volunteer clergy at Trinity; I taught, preached, celebrated Eucharist and led a study group in healing. I took some courses in massage and other hands-on healing arts. But most of all I wanted to work in a parish church. I love the liturgy, saying Mass and teaching children." Unfortunately, he died of AIDS before he could ever work for the Church he loved.

Georgeanne wants to be a priest. She hides her lesbianism. The bishop and the Commission on Ministry do not ask about her sexuality or personal life and so she is evaluated on paltry information. They, in an attempt to be fair, do not ask about sexuality and she is in the closet. Both lie. Both lose. What a shame and a sham on honesty and integrity. But that's the system, folks.

Ministry to and with homosexuals means to work to end discrimination in every institution in which it appears. This is a tall order, but this is the job that needs to be done.

Chapter 14. Effecting Change

All this is from God, who, through Christ, reconciled us to Himself and gave us a ministry of reconciliation.
                                    2 Corinthians 4:18

The time has come for the Church to admit past errors and bring reconciliation between homosexual people and the rest of the Body of Christ. The Church is all of us: clergy and lay people, straight and gay. We all have the duty to lead the Church into its appropriate course.

All of us try to live a life of good will. We often allow ourselves, however, our corners of hatred and bigotry. Following Christ's teaching of love is never easy. Both bigots and homosexuals are worthy of God's love and of ours. Jesus teaches us to pray for both the oppressed and the oppressor; self-righteousness, the hallmark of so many "Good Christians" today, is a convolution of Christ's teachings. We are all sinners. Homosexuals, their oppressors and those who idly watch as the oppression continues are all in need of God's forgiveness.

Are we willing to forgive up to seventy times seven? Are we ready to forgive ourselves for our hatred as we forgive those who from

In God's Image

their ignorance hate us and others? Can gays and their friends of good will be ready to pray for the souls of those who oppress them and to acknowledge their humanity?

But to pray and forgive does not mean allowing the oppression to continue. Persecutors, passive or virulent, must be held accountable for their words and actions, as we are held accountable for ours. Forgiveness does not mean looking the other way or putting up with injustice.

What can lesbian and gay male Episcopal lay people do to effect change?

First, you need to forgive yourselves for ever allowing the thought that you are not whole and healthy in God's eyes. You have been created in God's image and are responsible to live your life in truth and in love. You struggle, as we all struggle, to live God's role for us in co-creating all of life.

With the truth you will become fearless. You will find the strength to stand before the purple-clad bishops and declare that you are proud of your sexual orientation and demand full acceptance as a member of Christ's Church. When you know and proclaim that truth, no bishop will ever be able to stand between you and your calling as a Christian.

You must stand before the deputies to conventions as healthy whole people and demand that laws, rules, canons and resolutions be changed so that legal barriers affecting gay men and lesbians are dropped at every level of church life—marriage, ordination, teaching Sunday School, singing in choirs, serving as acolytes, etc. You will declare that full privileges in the church are your right by baptism and confirmation; you will remind the powers that the Book of Common Prayer does not issue a sexual preference questionnaire before it allows people to be baptized.

You must be willing to talk, educate, start dialogue and communicate with those who wish to continue to discriminate. As one conservative priest said to me recently, "I am not willing to have dialogue with them, because I am not willing to change my view that homosexuality is sinful." Such is the way of ignorance. But people of truth do not give up at the first hurdle.

Bear witness to your life as lover, friend, caring companion and gay man or lesbian. Take straight people to lunch and tell them who you are and how you behave and what you want. Tell them your story about discovering your sexual orientation, the problems and joys it has brought you. You have no idea how uninformed we straight people are about homosexual life. Your own personal story is your best educational tool.

Bear witness to your life as a Christian, a religious person. Attend church, receive the sacraments, say your prayers, visit the sick. Give money to the church. Share with your parish family what Jesus Christ and his ministry mean to you as a person and as a gay person. People need to know that people who have sex with others of the same gender also love God, worship and feel filled with the Holy Spirit. Socialize with the straight members of your parish even though they may be shy about being with an openly gay man or lesbian for the first time.

Dorothy Beattie served several years as president of Bay Area Integrity. She ran the national convention of Integrity in San Francisco in 1989. Integrity is the national organization of gay Episcopalians. Integrity has been responsible for keeping gay/lesbian concerns before the consciousness of the whole Episcopal Church.

A banker, now real estate agent, Dorothy has been on the forefront of gay/lesbian issues for many years. She personally bankrolled the 1989 Integrity convention, not only paying herself back, but contributing a sizable profit to the organization from her efforts. She was active in a largely lesbian parish in New York City, helping them through a financial crunch. Dorothy now attends Trinity in San Francisco.

Openly gay Episcopalians, like Dorothy, must speak and speak again, and not be afraid to go beyond education and dialogue, to exert pressure on the Church to bring about change. You cannot be afraid to exert pressure. Learn to use the media to your advantage.

Prejudice hates nothing more than the light of publicity. When injustice occurs in church, diocese or society, speak out. Learn to write media releases. Seek opportunities to appear on the radio and TV. Say things clearly, directly, succinctly. Take a strong stand. Don't be afraid to criticize people who attack you or other homosexuals. Get public. Frighten some people, it will help educate them and make them face the issues.

Several years ago there was much publicity when the bishop in San Francisco forbade the blessing of a homosexual relationship. Some clergy got together and in the Diocesan Convention passed a resolution calling for the Church to devise ceremonies for the blessings of gay and lesbian relationships. It also asked for services for the blessing of relationships between elderly people who could not marry because their social security income would be cut. Such a resolution could never have passed if it had not been for the negative publicity.

A television show in San Francisco wanted to host a debate between me and the bishop on the issue of the blessing of homosexual relationships. The bishop refused.

The Church hates and fears having its dirty linen washed in public. Good organization by oppressed groups can use that fear to bring about change and desired goals. The leadership of the Church hates to be forced to live by its own rules. The Church must be made to see itself as unloving, exclusive and failing in human kindness.

Organize groups of gay men, lesbians and straight fellow travelers. Get them to help you to be elected to offices (such as the vestry, the Diocesan Convention, the Synod, the General Convention) where you can exert pressure and make a witness for gay equality. Fight for your rights as a whole person and a Christian. This is not only your privilege, it is your responsibility.

In 1990 in the Convention of the Diocese of California, there was a resolution asking that the convention petition the President of the United States to issue an executive order forbidding discrimination against homosexual people in the armed forces. The good news is that it passed. The bad news is, that out of dozens of lesbians and gay men present, only two gay men spoke in support of the resolution.

Change comes about through pressure. There are many kinds of pressure to exert. You can go to meetings and conventions. You can write letters and articles. You can work on a one-to-one basis with individuals who have the power to effect change. Do not hesitate to plan events to confront church leadership when they pass legislation discriminating against gay and lesbian people. In the Bible, Jesus was not afraid to demonstrate his faith before the Pharisees. Have you not the courage to demonstrate before these contemporary Pharisees?

When the time is appropriate, lesbians and gay men have the right to organize and withhold money from the hierarchy of the churches in order to press for justice for homosexuals. You should love your oppressors but you need not support them financially. As the salaries and budgets of the bishops become pinched, they will discover ways to reconcile their beliefs with the wills of those that demand their respect.

Each year I ask the members of Trinity to give money to the church. I climb into the pulpit. I send letters. We make phone calls. We visit with people and ask them to contribute. It is ironic to me that people give so willingly and generously to an institution that ultimately uses that money to support measures that discriminate against them. The generosity of gay men and women is astonishing in light of how their money is used.

Frankly, I get annoyed that gay men and lesbians do not use their financial clout in the Church to bring about change. I detect a conservative, go-along-to-get-along attitude. At this present writing, our parish pays $32,000 a year to the Diocese of California. Three-quarters of that amount is from homosexuals. Yet the bishop does not push for full rights for gay and lesbian people in the Church.

The wealthy have always manipulated church leaders by opening and closing their checkbooks. Church leaders in the South failed to implement racial equality for fear of losing wealthy, entrenched members. Many dioceses in the South still have not publicly endorsed racial desegregation. Sadly, the course of the Church is still, too often, the course of the fattest wallet.

Finally, be impatient. Don't allow people to tell you to go slowly, be patient, wait, give it time. We Christians believe we are saved and justified right now by God's saving action in Christ. The job of reconciliation of homosexual people is already done in the action of Jesus Christ. Arrogant, discriminatory rules and narrow minds stand in the way of full freedom for gays and lesbians in our church and society "right now."

What can responsible straight members of the Church do to bring about justice for gay men and lesbians? One of my gay priest friends supports me by saying regularly to me that the witness of straight people for gay rights is the most important witness, because we have nothing to gain personally. There are as many closeted gay rights advocates among the straight members of the Church, however, as there are closeted gays. We fear we will be branded queer. Priests are afraid we will be passed over for better jobs in the Church. We fear we'll lose status, credibility and importance.

Here is vivid expression of Jesus' statement that if you lose your life you will find it. Anyone who has ever entered the arena of a battle for the rights of people has lost one kind of life and found a better one. I was an upwardly mobile star of a young priest on my way to be dean of a cathedral and then a bishop, until I was arrested in a civil rights demonstration. I became a gay rights advocate the following year. That may have ended my upward climb.

I was forced back to my own values, to deciding what was the important thing for me to do in my life. I lost the life of the social-climbing cleric. I found my life as an activist, rabble-rouser, lone eagle, writer, teacher, preacher, therapist and a priest. I don't have to go to boring cocktail parties, banquets, to give pious invocations, act the part of pseudo-socialite or fawn over the rich, hoping they'll donate money, and pretend to like it all. If I have lost the opportunity of my position as bishop, I have found my position as a server of Christ, an activist for social change.

There is a great act of faith in becoming an activist. The new life you find is a reflection of who you really are and what you really want. When you fight for the rights and freedoms of others, you discover the true meaning and importance of your own rights and freedoms.

The fight for the rights and freedom of homosexuals can't come from a patronizing attitude. This fight originates in the desire to become one with the oppressed. Reach out and touch the humanity of the many wonderful and vital people who are proud to say they are gay and Christian. Get beyond your own ignorance and lack of sensitivity and the truth will then become apparent, not as an option but as an obligation, to a person of good faith and a Christian.

Straight advocates must also find the best way to accomplish our work. Some of us are needed to work through the halls of legislation in Church and society. Others can be public activists—writing, appearing on TV and radio—letting the truth be known. Others can educate, telling our story of how we became advocates. We can introduce our gay friends to our other friends, our neighbors and our families. We can stop anti-gay jokes and stories in social situations. We can stand up for what we believe.

Deborah Franquist, married mother of three, has served for several years on the board of Integrity in the San Francisco Bay Area. A member of St. Aidan's Episcopal Church, she chose the board as a way of expressing the social outreach of that parish to the larger San Francisco community. Expressing in her life the tenets of her faith, Dorothy has educated herself and is teaching others.

There must be massive sex education for people to understand what homosexuality is and is not. Part of that education means bringing straight and gay persons into dialogue and creating communication. People need to know each other as individuals. "Take a faggot to lunch" is my motto. For as the Swahili proverb says, "If I do not know you, I do not value you."

I am a lone eagle. I do not hesitate to rabble-rouse; I write letters to editors, prepare articles and present resolutions to deanery meetings and diocesan conventions to force people to think about homosexual issues whether they want to or not. I seldom expect the resolutions to pass, but I do find they are successful in causing discomfort to those who continue to oppress gay/lesbian people by ignoring them or passing legislation against them. Out of this discomfort, such people often learn and change.

What can gay and lesbian clergy do to effect change? COME OUT OF THE CLOSET!

You can't be an open, honest, free person if you are hiding a basic part of your personhood and sexuality. How can you express love clearly if you can't talk about your lover or your sexuality?

Certainly, this is easy for me to say. I know that there are many important reasons why you choose to live this lie. In the long count, however, only the truth can make you free. Hiding in the closet makes you a slave.

Gay and lesbian clergy also need to tell their story. You can tell about the babies you've baptized, children you've taught, people you have visited in the hospital, weddings performed, the dead you have buried.

You can share the humiliation you felt when people told queer jokes in your presence. You can share the pain of going to social events and your lover could not come with you. You can tell of all the plays, TV shows, movies, magazine articles and radio programs that feature husband, wife and 2.3 children, but the gay and lesbian world is not acknowledged, is invisible or, even worse, stereotyped.

You can share your faith in God and Christ and your belief that God loves you and your love of people of the same gender as yourself. If half of the closeted clergy in the Episcopal Church had the courage to proclaim the truth and demand respect for both who they are and what they are, the barriers of ignorance that have stood for centuries would fall as quickly as the Berlin Wall.

The Rev. Malcolm Boyd came out of the closet in one of his many books and has long been a gay rights advocate. A freedom rider for black rights in the '60s, his passionate social concern moved quickly into the gay rights movement. He lectures, writes, preaches, appears on radio and television as an artist, a priest and an ardent activist. His book *Are You Running with Me, Jesus?* made Malcolm famous, and prayer exciting. He has changed the hearts and minds of millions by his witness to the humanity and dignity of gayness.

For gay/lesbian clergy already out of the closet, the largest responsibility falls on your shoulders. Your leadership and shining example as Christians is the clearest light we have for social change. As role models to the laity, your voices must be clear, positive and exuberant. Get political. Organize our many sympathetic and understanding brethren. Together we must make our voices heard in the halls of churchly legislation. Become part of a power group. Lose your life so you can find it.

Don't let the Church patronize you. Don't accept crumbs that fall from the bishop's table. Leaders will tell you they are working for your rights, then set up panels that have no gay or lesbian representation. Protest such flagrancy. Insist on being placed in important jobs in parishes and missions. Many bishops will say they will help and don't. Have the courage to hold them to task. Remember *you are the Church;* so are we all. Don't let them use your time, talents and money to deprive you of your rights.

The Rev. Bernard Mayes, a gay priest of the Episcopal Church founded The Parsonage in San Francisco in the '70s. A decade earlier he had founded San Francisco Suicide Prevention. Bernie worked professionally for KQED-television. He was a broadcast and communications expert. He now teaches communications in Virginia.

The Parsonage is in a Victorian cottage located behind commercial property in the city's primarily gay Castro District. A red, white and blue sign "The Episcopal Church Welcomes You" marks the entry. Originally The Parsonage was developed to deal with gay youngsters who were coming into the city in huge numbers. Today the group is dedicated to educating the new bishop who came in 1979 on gay and lesbian issues.

The Rev. Prof. W. Norman Pittenger taught at the General Theological Seminary in New York City for 25 years. His was a sacred and liberal theology that showed students how to make Christianity relevant to the world. After his retirement from GTS, he went to King's College Cambridge in England and taught there for another 20 years.

When Ann and I visited him in the summer of 1990, he was well into his eighties. Sharp, funny and concerned, he despaired of the growing conservatism in England on homosexual issues. He had come out 15 years earlier and wrote a fine pamphlet "Homosexuality and the Church" which has been widely distributed. I cannot keep enough copies on the literature rack at Trinity.

What can bishops do to effect change? Learn to see gay men and lesbians as human beings. They are not pawns in a religio-political game of the good guys against the bad guys. Bigotry and judgment cannot justly hide behind a position of authority—your obligation is to the love of Christ, not your own self-righteousness. "Those who do unto the least, do unto me." Were the teachings of Jesus given in vain?

As honest Christians, you must become advocates of the rights of all people. You must open your eyes to see that homosexuals are the last minority discriminated against in the laws of Church and state. Laws against Native Americans, blacks, Asians, Mexicans and Puerto Ricans have been stricken from the books. Only homosexuals are discriminated against in the laws, canons and resolutions of Church and society. You *must* recognize this sin and see to its immediate correction.

In times to come, those bishops who now vote against homosexual rights will feel just as foolish as do those bishops who voted against civil rights legislation for blacks in the 1960s. Homosexuals are not going to go away.

Bishops should make sure that parishes and missions in all

jurisdictions insist on education and dialogue concerning gay rights. We have passed resolutions about such activity with precious little action on the local level.

Bishops must liberate the Bible from the hands of tyrants who use it to oppress homosexuals and others. Episcopalians are not biblical fundamentalists and idolizers. On every other issue, we interpret the Bible as a work of love and compassion, yet when it comes to arguments against homosexuals, bishops, priests and lay people become one-issue, instant fundamentalists. They quote Deuteronomy and Paul with the same vigor and dogmatism as does the Rev. Jerry Falwell. This is dirty pool and sleazy Christianity.

Bishops have a wide variety of people to please in their dioceses. Conservatives, liberals, moderates and rights activists all want the bishop to listen to their banging drum. Issues of justice, however, are crystal clear. Full rights and freedoms for women, the elderly, racial and ethnic groups, and homosexuals ought to be clear-cut issues for Americans and certainly for Christians.

Bishops can place and recommend gay and lesbian clergy for job openings in their dioceses. They can keep their word when they say they will ordain homosexual clergy. They can educate the lay people who call clergy to positions so that they will examine with an open mind candidates who are gay. They must use the power of the office to humanize the selection process.

A very few bishops have done a splendid job in effecting change in the Church. Three names come to mind, all of whom are married men and I have no reason to think they are anything but straight.

The Rt. Rev. Paul Moore was bishop of New York in the '70s and '80s. He has long been an outspoken advocate of gay and lesbian rights. He ordained the Rev. Ellen Barrett, a lesbian, to the priesthood in 1977. There was a great furor in the Church at the time. The Church calmed down. Moore also got the Church thinking about the rights of gay and lesbian parents.

The Rt. Rev. John Spong, Bishop of Newark, NJ, not only ordained an openly gay man, the Rev. Robert Williams, but has also called for the Church to permit the blessing of same-sex unions. He has been a courageous advocate of these issues in the House of Bishops and on national television. He has written several books with a very liberal view of theology and human sexuality. He has made many in the Church furious and he has made us think.

The Rt. Rev. George Hunt is the the bishop of Rhode Island. Starting as a middle-of-the-road conservative, he has become a compassionate caring advocate of gay/lesbian rights. He heads a commission of the Church investigating all aspects of human sexuality. He is quietly and clearly changing attitudes of leaders throughout the Church.

But those who speak and act remain few. Those who sit pompous and closed-minded with their prejudices unchallenged are legion. The time to act has come. Bishops and all Christians must act valiantly in the name of the one who offered salvation to *all* humankind.

There will be people in the Church who will be distressed, for you will be affronting their bigotry and self-righteousness. But this is a small price to pay for what you can do to to help rebuild the Church as a loving haven for all of God's children. It is time to relieve the hurt of those whom we have hurt for so very long. The process of reconciliation needs to include all people. We cannot allow those who choose to discriminate to dominate the Church of love and peace and reconciliation.

"Not without each other" is a statement by theologian the Rev. Prof. Rowan Williams that sums up the fight against homosexism. Clergy and lay people, gays, lesbians and straights are in the fight for human rights together. Nothing much will happen without each other. Everything will happen as we work together.

There is no such thing as Jew and Greek, slave and free, male and female, [gay and straight,] for you are all one person in Christ Jesus.

Galatians 3:38

Index

Baldwin, James 16
Barrett, the Rev. Ellen 123
Beattie, Dorothy 115
Bishop of California 30, 66, 116
Book of Common Prayer 44, 45, 57, 114
Boyd, the Rev. Malcolm 120
Britt, Harry 86
Brown vs. the Board of Education 15
Browning, Bishop Edmund 29
Bush, President George 66, 86
Catton, Bruce 23
child molesting 73-75
Conv. of the Diocese of Cal., 1988 66
Conv. of the Diocese of Cal., 1990 116
Council on Religion & the Homosexual 17
Cromey, the Rev. Edwin 39
cross-dressing 80-81
Falwell, the Rev. Jerry 64, 123
Federal Lesbians And Gays 85
Feinstein, Mayor Dianne 65
Fellows of the College of Preachers, D.C. Conference 29
Frank, Congressman Barney 86
Franquist, Deborah 119
Gallup poll 49
Gay Episcopal clergy 31, 120-122
General Conference of the Methodist Church, 1988 30
General Convention of the Episcopal Church, 1988 30
General Convention of the Episcopal Church, 1991 66
General Theological Seminary, NYC 15, 24, 69, 122
"Geraldo" 13
Glide Foundation, S.F. 17
Grace Cathedral, S.F. 16, 61
Hayden, Sterling 16
Holy Eucharist 25, 102
homophobia, *(definition of)* 22
homosexuality, as an act of free choice 75-76
homosexuals 30
 blessing relationships of 30-32, 39-45, 50, 66
 gender role playing of 81-82
 ordination of 31-32, 108
 promiscuity 77-80
House of Bishops, 1987 report 91
Huddleston, the Rev. Trevor 15
Hudson, Rock 62
Hunt, Bishop George 124
Integrity 115, 119
Jesus, biblical teachings of 23, 43, 47-48, 50, 113, 117, 118, 122
John Paul II, Pope, statement on homosexuality 22
King, Jr., the Rev. Dr. Martin Luther 16
Kowalski, Sharon 88

125

Lambeth Conference, 1978 107
Lattin, Don 42
Lay Academy, Diocese of California 91
Leibowitz, Fran 90
"Let's Make A Deal" 91
Lincoln, Abraham 24
Lion's Club, gay 90
masturbation 36, 47, 50, 61, 75
Mayes, the Rev. Bernard 121
Milk, Harvey 85
Moore, Bishop Paul 123
Moral Majority 64
Mormon Church, homophobia of 68-69
NAACP 16
National Commission on AIDS 66
New Testament
    Corinthians 113
    Galatians 124
    justification of slavery 23
    teachings on homosexuality 22, 36
Newsweek 64
Old Testament
    Adam and Eve 24
    charging interest condemned 23
    Deuteronomy 123
    Jonathan and David 44
    teaching on fabrics of mixed sources 36
    teachings on adultery 36
    teachings on homosexuality 22, 36, 47
Pittenger, the Rev. Prof. W. Norman 122
Reagan, President Ronald 62, 65
San Francisco Chronicle 86
San Francisco Examiner 42
sin 54, 55-58
Spong, Bishop John 123
St. Aidan's Episcopal Church, S.F. 119
St. Paul's Episcopal School, NY 15
Swing, the Rt. Rev. William E. 30
Sydney, Australia Anglical Diocese 30
teenage suicide, congr. study on 87
The Parsonage, S.F. 92, 121
Thompson, Karen 88
Time 64
transsexuality 81
U.S. Armed Services, homophobia in the 86
Williams, the Rev. Prof. Rowan 124
Williams, the Rev. Robert 123

Also from . . .   ALAMO SQUARE PRESS

Being • Being Happy • Being Gay
Pathways to a Rewarding Life for Lesbians and Gay Men

by Bert Herrman

"His observations are as clear and lucid as his prose, his message simple but direct: This is a time to not only survive but to thrive. Being gay is a gift, and certainly an ever unfolding mystery. Herrman extends a compassionate and useful hand in the journey toward realizing our full human potential." — Mark Thompson, Senior Editor, *The Advocate*

For your copy, send a check for $8.00 (publisher covers postage, handling and sales tax, if applicable) and mail to:

ALAMO SQUARE PRESS
P.O. Box 14543
San Francisco, CA 94114